# RANGE RATS

D0863306

*How to get your swing from*

*the practice range*

*to the golf course*

# RANGE RATS

*How to get your swing from the practice range
to the golf course*

## BY ROGER MALTBIE

### with RON SALSIG

Woodford Press

Printed in Appleton, Wisconsin.

Designed by Jim Santore, Woodford Press.
Edited by Dave Burgin.

Woodford Press
5900 Hollis Street, Suite K
Emeryville, CA 94608
(510) 985-0675
www.woodfordpub.com

Library of Congress Catalog Card Number: 99-65700.

ISBN: 0-942627-58-x

C. David Burgin, Editor and Publisher
Dan Ross, CEO and Publisher
William F. Duane, Esq., Vice President

Photography by David Lilienstein and Jim Santore.

Associate Publishers:
Franklin M. Dumm
William B. McGuire, Esq.
William W. Scott, Esq.
Gary Notti, CPA

# Dedication

For Donna and our sons, Spencer and Parker. And for mom and dad, Joan and Lin Maltbie

# Acknowledgments

No career in golf can be noteworthy without the help of many people. At least that notion certainly is true in my case. The game of golf seems endlessly enjoyable with never-ending challenges. I have met so many fascinating people who have taught me and supported me — friends and fans who have shared my experiences over the years. Thank you, one and all.

In my junior days it was Eddie Duino, head professional at San Jose (California) Country Club for nearly 40 years, who cared enough to answer a kid's relentless questioning. Eddie's lessons were not restricted to golf, either.

Thanks galore to those who walked me through my career on the Tour — Frank Pieper, David Larson, Jeff Burrell, Mike Boyce and Dave Quesenberry.

Many thanks to Barny Hinkle, Michele Bagwell and all the folks at Michelob, the company that has loyally sponsored me since 1981.

Lou Ortiz and Richard On made the golf clubs I used as a kid. It is still Orlimar clubs I play, thanks to Jessie Ortiz, Ed Dolinar and Rich Oldenburg.

I dearly love working for NBC in telecasting men's and women's golf events. Tommy Roy, Dick Ebersol and the crew at NBC have helped me enormously. What a learning experience it has been. I am fortunate indeed. My agent, John Mascatello, and his assistant, Kim Donovan, and the gang in his office get my vote any day.

No thank-you is big enough for Peter Kostis, who helped put back together the pieces of my shattered golf game after the death of Eddie Duino in 1977. The countless hours Peter has given me for no more compensation than a thank-you — I am forever in his debt.

A special thanks to Ken Venturi for his college scholarship, wisdom, tutelage and, most important, his friendship. Other golf coaches who helped to shape my life as I was growing up in Northern California are Chon Gallegos at James Lick High School, Harley Dow at San Jose City College and Jerry Vroom at San Jose State University. A foursome of wonderful men.

Frankly, I have thought for quite a while that I just might have a book in me. So here it is, thanks to Woodford Press of Emeryville, California. Woodford's editor and publisher Dave Burgin came up with the unique "Range Rats" idea. As presented by Dave, the idea instantly captured my imagination over lunch at the Olympic Club with Dave and his Woodford partner, Dan Ross.

Thanks go to Paul Kennedy and Jim Lucius, general manager and head professional, respectively, at historic Olympic, site of four U.S. Opens. They warmly permitted us to use their practice tee — a Range Rat heaven — for picture-taking and, well, Range Ratting.

At that same lunch was Ron Salsig. I have known Ron a long time from the Bay Area golf wars. He has impressively made the transition from player to golf writer, but not without a tough struggle. For that, and for making something coherent out of my thoughts for this book, Ron has my gratitude and respect.

# Yes, They Found His Check

Roger Maltbie is a five-time winner on the PGA Tour who has endeared himself to golfers around the world for his lively, common-sense approach to explaining the game of golf to TV audiences as an analyst for NBC Sports.

Maltbie established himself as a player in his first year on Tour, 1975, with back-to-back wins in the Quad Cities Open and the Pleasant Valley Classic. He also earned a reputation as a colorful personality while capturing Rookie of the Year honors with a very human error after winning his second title in Boston.

He lost the first-place check in a bar that night. A janitor found the check on the floor the next morning. Roger eventually got his money, but he also had a new image.

His next win also came in colorful fashion — in 1976 in the inaugural Memorial Tournament created by Jack Nicklaus. Maltbie hit a gallery post well over the 17th green on the third hole of a three-hole playoff with Hale Irwin. The ball kicked back onto the green close to the pin, enabling him to extend the playoff to the 18th hole, where he made birdie to win the title.

In 1985 Maltbie also won twice with victories in the Westchester Classic and the World Series of Golf. In the 1987 Masters Maltbie finished one stroke out of a playoff (which Larry Mize won by sinking a pitch shot from the right side of the 11th green). Roger also won the 1980 Magnolia Classic, an unofficial title played opposite the Masters.

Maltbie began playing golf by sneaking onto the nearby San Jose Country Club in California with his brother, John. He got to know the head pro, Eddie Duino, in a hurry. Maltbie's father, Lin, soon joined the club and the family has played there ever since.

Duino was Maltbie's golf teacher for the next 20 years.

As was true of most promising young players in Northern California around that time — for example, Johnny Miller and Tony Lema — Maltbie grew up playing Orlimar golf clubs. He has remained friends over the years with Lou Ortiz, owner of Orlimar Golf Company, and in 1997 became an investor in and spokesman for the Bay Area-based firm.

Maltbie was inducted into the California Golf Writers Hall of Fame in 1986. In his acceptance speech at Pebble Beach, he noted he was a lifelong fan of the San Francisco 49ers, not knowing that 49ers owner Eddie DeBartolo was in the audience. The two became good friends, and Maltbie now owns three Super Bowl rings.

In 1989, NBC asked Maltbie to join its golf broadcasting team, but he declined so he could continue to compete full-time on the Tour. After two shoulder surgeries, in 1991 he finally took the job as the golf analyst for NBC.

Maltbie lives in the San Jose suburb of Los Gatos with his family.

# Hello, Golf!

The first time I saw Roger Maltbie swing a golf club, I knew I was looking at something special. Rhythmic and fluid, his swing seemed so uncomplicated, yet produced such power.

Maltbie was hitting golf balls that day about three stalls down from me on the driving range at Spyglass Hill Golf Course, just up the slope from Pebble Beach. We were both unwinding from second-round wins in a match play tournament, the 1972 Northern California Golf Association Championship.

Whimsically, I began copying his motion. Although I had won my match, I had lost my swing. Again. Actually, I never had a swing I could really call my own. I just borrowed others. Maltbie had the best swing on the range, so I thought I would try his — as best as I could duplicate it, anyway.

It wasn't just his swing that captured my attention and respect. Maltbie had a jovial way of carrying himself that, coupled with his mesmerizing swing tempo, somehow made the entire game look easy.

On the range he would banter with friends until dusk. On the course he had a good time, while guys like me kept grinding it out. I could only wonder what the game was like for players like Roger Maltbie. I had seen golfers like him before, and I longed for the day the game would be so simple. And so much fun, apparently. How did he do it? There had to be a secret.

I lost my next match and went home to practice. Roger won the tournament.

Practice in golf is done on a driving range, a field of dreams if ever there was one. Ah, sweet mysteries of golf! How they do enthrall.

And that is how, early on, I became a Range Rat, a guy dreaming of that one day when everything would come together in one beautiful package, the swing mystery solved and the game made easier. And I could walk from the practice tee to the first tee with confidence.

Through all my experimenting I had developed skills enough to play for the University of California at Berkeley golf team. I played at Cal at the same time Gary McCord played for UC Riverside, and at the same time a guy by the name of Tom Watson played for Stanford. (I beat Watson once — he shot 86. I'll spare you the details.)

Then one day I caught a glimpse of the magic. While in graduate school studying "The History of Ideas" (an ideal preoccupation for any golf theorist), I entered a Monday morning qualifier for a PGA Tour event, the old Kaiser Open in Napa, California. This was the fall of 1972. I managed to birdie four of the final six holes for a 72, earning an alternate spot in the tournament.

Alternates were allowed on the range at the tournament site, a Range Rat's Nirvana. On Tuesday, I recognized Lee Trevino's swing down at the other end of the range. I knew he was a bonafide Range Rat, and his constant jabbering made me think he was accessible. I dropped my bucket of balls near his, and begged, "Help!"

"I watched you over there," Trevino cackled. "You need it."

Trevino watched me hit balls for an hour, explaining his ideas and secrets and applying them to my swing. I had never hit the ball better in my life. I was astounded. Hello, golf! From a train wreck to swing euphoria in one day!

It didn't last, of course. Neither did my dream of becoming a PGA Tour professional. Many of the guys I played against in college were already out there — Watson, McCord and my teammate at Cal, Artie McNickle. All I really did as a pro was make it to Stage II qualifying for the Tour a couple of times and make the cut at a U.S. Open.

Roger Maltbie was dazzling on the Tour in his rookie year, 1975, winning twice. And he still made it look so easy.

That side of Roger is manifest to this day. His confident ease with people, his storytelling wit and charm, and his riveting ability to discuss the most complex aspects of the game in plain, common-sense terms — all this makes him great fun to be around.

The idea for this book came from Dave Burgin, legendary former newspaper editor who now is editor and co-publisher of Woodford Press. Before a medical condition cut in, Dave could have been the poster child for Range Ratting. He claims that more than once he has taken all three meals on the range.

A 1-handicap at the Olympic Club in San Francisco and Columbia CC in Chevy Chase, Maryland, Dave collected a few scalps in his day. "I won the Poor Robert's Open three times," Burgin boasts. "For me, that's three majors."

Dave and I were mulling over the names of several well-known players — men, women, seniors — who fit the Range Rat profile and who could write this book. "I've got it," I blared at last. "He's perfect! Roger Maltbie!" So perfect, in fact, you might say Roger wrote the book on Range Ratting. And this is it.

"Range Rat" is no derogation. The label is a badge of honor. To be a Range Rat is to be a member of a special golf subculture. It is to be among those people who love the game so much they feel they live in celebration of the game, its spirit, its creed. Jim Lucius, head professional at the Olympic Club, a true Range Rat and a terrific teacher, tells golfers on Olympic's spectacular range, "Welcome to my office."

Range Rats hit golf balls until backs ache and hands hurt. They kibitz and exchange ideas about the game, or offer tips they got from lessons or out of *Golf Digest* and *Golf* magazines. A Range Rat thinks he knows how to practice well. And what he doesn't know he will drop everything else to learn.

You won't ever see a true Range Rat racing to the practice tee, snatching his driver from his bag and, with no warm-ups, start swinging like a guy trapped in a phone booth with a wasp. A true Rat will stay until nightfall, then go to the putting green and practice by the light from the pro shop.

This book is for Range Rats everywhere, golfers from both genders, all ages and all levels of skill — wonderful people chasing the magic. And this book is for anyone, Range Rat or not, who has trouble getting his or her swing and game from the practice tee to the first tee. As Roger will tell you, that problem is not unknown to men and women on the pro Tours.

I am honored to be able to assist Roger in writing this book. We have had fun putting it together. This book is entirely about practice and getting the most out of practicing. It is about how to get your swing "across the road" to the first tee. There are no drawings about how to hold the club or where to place your feet on a downhill lie, no silly gimmicks like swinging with a broom or strapping on some weird shoulder contraption.

This book is the real answer to golf's most enduring question, "What is the best way for me really to improve my game?" The answer to that question is roughly the same answer the aging hippie gave to the rube on Fifth Avenue who asked how to get to Carnegie Hall: "Practice, man, practice."

Roger is not going to bombard you with breakthrough methods and secrets. There are hundreds of illustrated-to-death golf instruction books with as many different methods, but that's not what this book is about. The simple fact of the matter is that Tour pros like Roger have known how to practice this game for some time, but that knowledge somehow has never made it down to the golf-playing public. That is a surprising fact, really.

I cannot ever recall seeing an important golf book devoted exclusively to practice, as this one is. We are going to ask you to figure out for yourself what to practice, what you need to work on. This book will direct you to your own deficiencies. And then you hit the range.

Included on these pages are detailed charts very much like the charts the Tours supply for their players. Chart every shot you hit (focused golfers have no trouble remembering every shot, right?) over as few as 10 rounds, and then you can analyze your deficiencies and trouble spots. And then you practice accordingly.

For example, if you are driving the ball in the fairway consistently, but you can't hit greens in regulation, you would probably conclude you need to work on your iron game. Of course.

Sometimes it's not so obvious — have you ever counted up how many times you use a sand wedge in a round? Most golfers who have poor putting rounds figure out they need to hit the putting green for an hour. Why should ball-striking, including the wedge game, be any different?

Roger will tell you how to use these charts. Take pains with them. Then work on your shortcomings as they become apparent. You will be amazed at how the consistency of "mistakes" pop out at you from the charts. And if you work hard, maybe take a lesson or two, you also will be amazed at how fast you improve. Guaranteed!

The fun comes when you get your swing and game from the range to the golf course. That is the upshot of practicing intelligently. In golf, as Roger explains on the ensuing pages, it is not practice that makes perfect, but PERFECT PRACTICE THAT MAKES PERFECT.

# World-class Range Rats

In this book is a special piece by Bill Scott, for many years a competitive amateur player in the Washington, D.C. area. Bill, a lawyer, is an investor in Woodford Press and a long-time friend of Dave Burgin, Woodford's editor and publisher.

It is strictly unofficial, but we believe Bill holds the world record for either the most number of lessons taken by an amateur or the most lessons taken from the most professionals. Or both.

Bill Scott is kind of an Eagle Scout of Range Ratting, holding enough merit badges for several troops. He knows his ranges. Bill's friends claim he has spent enough money on golf lessons to buy Augusta National. You will enjoy his story.

Shannon Rouillard, a former captain of the women's golf team at the University of Oregon, is now a golf coach at the school. A former professional at Palo Alto Hills Golf and Country Club, south of San Francisco, Shannon has played in the Women's U.S. Open. And she is a staunch Range Rat, as she articulates nicely later in the book.

# Chapter 1

## LEARN HOW TO PRACTICE . . .
## THE '21-DAYS' RULE . . .
## BEN HOGAN'S SECRET . . .
## BEWARE: RATZILLA IS COMING . . .

As is true for most Tour pros, I'm often asked questions about the golf swing. I don't mind at all. This is a tough game, and if I can lighten anyone's burden, I welcome the opportunity.

But when I talk with these golfers, more often than not I find that the problems they encounter have little to do with the golf swing. The problem is with the way they practice.

A man came up to me at a benefit tournament for junior golf with an exasperated look in his eyes and told me he had been playing this game for years, but he just did not seem to be getting anywhere. He needed advice on his swing, he said.

I told him that if he was looking for a magic lamp to rub, he was talking to the wrong cowboy, because I ran out of genies somewhere around my second year on Tour. But I was more than happy to help, so I asked him what he was working on in practice. He shook his head and said it must be the wrong thing.

I asked him if he had looked at his fundamentals. He half-smiled and said he had seen videos of his swing. He said his stance was all screwed up — the feet are lined up way out to the right and his shoulders dead left. But every time he tried to correct the problem the ball went all over the place and he just can't stand it anymore. He needed to start over. A whole new swing, he said.

Well, I leaned back and told him his problem wasn't at all in his swing. The problem was in his practice sessions. He gave me that goofy look I always see whenever I mention the problem might be in the way a golfer practices this game.

Mike Sica builds a "station" with a club on the ground and an old broken shaft stuck into the turf to facilitate alignment. More about this subject in Chapter 3.

Of course the ball goes all over the place! I told him that when any golfer works on a new position or technique in the golf swing, it always destroys rhythm and tempo. Every time.

When the practice session involves learning a new position, the goal is not where the ball goes. The goal is learning a new position, creating a new habit. I say it takes a figurative "21 days" to learn a new position, to create a new habit in the golf swing. For 21 days you simply cannot care where the ball goes. And that is that.

I explained to him that learning a swing position (hands position, takeaway, turn, etc.) was only one of two distinct kinds of practice sessions. The other practice session is all about getting your game from the practice tee to the golf course. In that session, the only concern is target and ball flight, where the ball goes. Nothing else, just target and flight.

I could tell by his lost expression that he was hearing all this for the first time. I had seen that look too many times before. I decided right there that someday I would write a book about how to practice this game, what to do when you buy that bucket of balls at your local range and go to work on your game.

Book stores are filled with books on golf instruction. Most explain how to grip the club, how to swing the golf club, and the like. The fundamentals of this game are pretty well covered.

But a funny thing happens when it comes to practice — it is taken for granted. These books all tell the reader they must practice these things diligently. Usually it's no more than a footnote. Gee, thanks, you mean you have to practice this new swing? You have to practice to improve! What insight!

But no book has been written on how to practice. None that I can recall, anyway.

It has always bothered me how little the average golfer knows about practice. With the mountains of instructional material available to the general public, practically nothing has reached the average golfer about the most important aspect of any attempt to improve — how to practice what they're learning.

Let's start by identifying the two practice sessions in golf. I call them Practice A and Practice B. I also call Practice A "practicing golf," and I call Practice B "practicing the swing."

Practice A is all about practicing the game itself, practicing golf the way it is played on the golf course. That may seem pretty straightforward at first glance, but I was on Tour a decade before I learned anything about this practice (A) session.

Practice B is the practice session golfers are most familiar with, but that does not mean they know how to do it. This type of practice is all about learning a position in the golf swing, incorporating a swing fundamental, creating a new habit. It is technical practice, mechanical practice, the kind of practice that has a golfer hitting balls well into the night, and again at daybreak.

The problem with far too many golfers is they mix up these two practice sessions. You have to know what to expect from each, how to use each.

I am constantly amazed at the number of golfers I run into who are not familiar with the unwritten rules of practice. On Tour, we've known these rules for some time. Somehow the news just has never filtered down to the rest of the golf world. Not even glassy-eyed old Range Rats know.

I told my new friend that he was mixing up the two distinct practice sessions, and *that* was the problem. His goal was to create a new habit. But he was gauging his progress on where the ball was going. His practice session (what I call Practice B) had nothing to do with where the ball went. Practice A has to do with where the ball goes. Practice B does not.

By working on a swing position and getting frustrated with where the ball was going, he had broken the cardinal rule of serious practicing, which is keeping those two practice sessions separate.

**Professional Shannon Rouillard usually spends the whole day on the range, either teaching or practicing.**

16

I explained further that he had broken another rule of practice by expecting results right away. When the ball started going all over the place, he was convinced he was working on the wrong thing. He gave up on his new stance and tried something else. Before he knew it he was doing guesswork, the great destroyer of all practice sessions. That is the danger. When you start practicing guesswork, you're toast.

I told him how he practiced is every bit as important as what he practiced. The contest is not the number of balls hit, it is the quality of work accomplished. I told him to expect the ball to go everywhere while he was creating a habit. Stick with it. Over time, he had to see the results.

"Nobody's ever told me there was a way to practice," my new friend said. "What else do you guys know about practice that guys like me have never heard before?"

Well, it took me more than a decade on Tour to learn how to practice, so how could I fault my new buddy? He looked at me and said he would like to ask a favor. He said there are a lot of kids out here, and they all hit a lot of balls every day. Real Range Rats. Would I explain to them what Tour pros know about practice?

Now I couldn't resist that one. If they listened, I might be able to save those teenagers a lot of the anguish I went through in learning this game. One thing for sure about Range Rats — they love to spread the knowledge. It's part

> ## PRACTICE A — PRACTICING GOLF (TARGET, FLIGHT) . . .
>
> - THINK TARGET AND BALL FLIGHT.
> - THINK RHYTHM, TEMPO AND BALANCE.
> - NO THOUGHTS ABOUT SWING POSITIONS.
> - THINK "OUT THERE," NOT "IN HERE."
> - STICK WITH YOUR STYLE, THE WAY YOU HIT THE BALL.
> - ELIMINATE GUESSWORK.
> - ALWAYS USE PRACTICE A TO CARRY YOU FROM THE RANGE TO THE GOLF COURSE.

of the culture. If those teenagers were real Range Rats, that message would spread like a good report card.

On the pages that follow, I will explain how I learned the correct way to practice this game. In the process I will give a history of practice and how it evolved.

Practice is wasted time if a golfer isn't working on the right things. What we do on Tour is chart out our rounds, so we know where our game is lacking. It is our way of taking inventory. Then we know what we have to work on in our practice sessions. In this book I have included charts not unlike the ones we use on Tour so the reader will also know what part of his game needs work.

Anyone who has ever picked up a golf

When a true Range Rat dreams, he dreams by the bucket . . .

club has had the experience of finding something in this or her swing on the range that works, but somehow that same thing will not work on the golf course. On the first tee, that same swing suddenly sends the ball sideways.

Baffling, isn't it? It is as if there is an invisible wall somewhere in those few yards between the range and the first tee. I have certainly had the experience. But I've found a few ways to carry that swing from the range to the first tee.

Ben Hogan was once asked what his secret really was, and he told that man to go dig it out of the ground as he had. There is a lot of truth there — to learn this game, you must practice. To play this game well, to play it to the best of your ability, all it takes is hard work. There's nothing that about 200 buckets of balls won't cure. LARGE buckets.

But somewhere, at some unspecified point in time, we lost track of our priorities. Hit a thousand balls the wrong way and you've accomplished nothing. Indeed, you may grooved a mistake.

But how do you practice?

When it comes right down to it, there's only one person who really has the right to know. He's looked at as an obsessive, grunt-of-the-earth kind of guy, a little quirky in personality. It's a Range Rat. Curious breed.

The Range Rats of the world are not a celebrated bunch. A Range Rate is not the popular conception of a golfer. But we RRs are the backbone of golf, the commoners who truly celebrate the culture while at the same time creating its lore

and advancing the knowledge. After all, we are out there in the laboratory, although it perhaps has more the look of a neighborhood playground.

Range Rats have always existed in the game of golf, but the Age of the Rat is upon us now. Practice has never been so popular. Driving ranges are popping up all over the world, most state-of-the-art. Now they're called practice facilities. The culture is growing like some giant sci-fi creature oozing up out of the ground.

## PRACTICE B — PRACTICING SWING (POSITIONS, BASICS) . . .

- DON'T WORRY WHERE THE BALL GOES.
- ALWAYS HAVE A PRACTICE PLAN.
- OBJECTIVE IS TO CREATE SOMETHING TECHNICAL IN SWING.
- REPEAT NEW POSITION UNTIL YOU BEGIN TO FEEL PROGRESS.
- IT TAKES 21 DAYS OF WORK TO CREATE A HABIT.
- FUNDAMENTAL POSITIONS MUST BE PRACTICED, TOO.
- DON'T MIX PRACTICE A WITH PRACTICE B.
- BUILD A STATION (ALIGNMENT AND BALL POSITION).
- DON'T MESS WITH YOUR STYLE, YOUR "THUMB PRINT."
- FIND A PRO WHO WILL WORK WITH YOUR STYLE.

19

It's Range Ratzilla!

Range Rats are everywhere these days. And, I confess, I am one. These are my people. This is my place.

I have always thought it is the best part of the Tour.

Practice has changed significantly on Tour in my time. We've learned a great deal. It shows in the way the current generation of golfers play the game. Scores have never been lower. Not just the winning scores, everybody's score.

Sure, the equipment is better and the courses are immaculate. But you've still got to hit the ball, and these guys are all better at it than any generation before them. It's not because they have a secret. It's because of the way they practice the game.

We just haven't told you about it. Time to share the knowledge.

Oh, I'll throw in a few stories along the way. Wouldn't be a Range Rat if I didn't.

"RANGE RATS"

# Chapter 2

## 'PRACTICE A' IS FOR THE GOLF COURSE . . . FEAR AND LOATHING AT THE MASTERS . . . HOLD THAT 'THUMB PRINT'. . .

Pure golf is fickle and fleeting. "It" — pure golf — just doesn't seem to hang around long, no matter who you are, no matter how good your swing may have felt yesterday or last week. And when "it" takes a hike, hello humility.

Losing "it" is something every golfer has experienced at one time or another. Sad testimony to that fact is the veritable junkyard of snapped shafts in the tee-box waste cans, the putters and wedges at the bottom of lakes and ponds. I remember once a Tour pro named Bill Malley threw his whole bag into a lake and walked right off the course. Late that night, Malley was seen wading back into that lake to retrieve his car keys. The bag and clubs he left in their watery grave. Bruce Crampton summed it up best. He said if you never played poorly you would never learn anything. And knowledge can come at the most unexpected time, as it did for me at the 1987 Masters.

It is always a thrill to drive up Magnolia Lane and stop your car in front of the clubhouse at Augusta National, one of those magic moments in golf. And you hope the magic rubs off.

But when I parked the car in 1987, that magic jumped out and hitched a ride to Atlanta, for all I know. I had no idea where the ball was going. By the time I got to the golf course my bag was a country club for evil spirits.

This was not a good time to lose "it," just before the Masters. But I had lost it, no question. Truth to tell, I knew it long before I flew to Augusta. I was just hoping for a miracle. Didn't have to be a big miracle, either. A minor one would do.

Well, miracles do happen, but you

just can't ever bet on them. Little did I know I was about to learn the most important lesson in my practicing life. Actually, I was about to learn *how* to practice. Period. I wouldn't say I knew a whole lot about the subject before that 1987 Masters.

My miseries began when my instructor, Peter Kostis, gave me a move to work on in my takeaway. And it took away everything. He wanted me to keep my hands inside the club path going away from the ball, to keep the clubhead out so I didn't tangle myself up and trip all over myself on the backswing. I was working hard on that. Too hard.

By the time I got to the range at Augusta, "it" was in complete meltdown. Every ball I hit went left or right. I had no clue. Big-time guessing game.

Peter came by to check me out, and quickly kind of looked down at the ground and shook his head. He took a deep breath and told me to stop hitting balls. Then he tried to explain something to me.

He told me I was playing golf swings, not playing golf. He said that I was playing golf with a practice mentality, trying to make good golf swings. He said my swing wasn't as bad as I thought it was, and the things we had been working on were basically there in the swing. He told me that now I had to go back to playing golf and let those things show through.

I kind of stood there dumbfounded, not exactly sure what he was talking about.

"You know what you are doing?" Peter said. "You're going out there on the golf course and you're playing practice swing. You're playing practice. You're not playing golf. Forget thinking about how you're taking the club away from the ball. You've done that. You've done the time, you've done your due diligence. You've made the correction, so now go back to trying to shape the shots as you would want to on the golf course. Think *golf* again."

He told me that he was not going to work on my golf swing anymore, thank you. He said all we were going to work on was the pace of my swing. Timing, rhythm, balance. That's it. That's all we're going to think about.

I was like, "Excuse me?"

I mean, he was looking at a very serious train wreck here. Couldn't he see that? We had to piece this thing back together again somehow. And in a hurry.

Let's just say there was a considerable degree of apprehension on my part to try this thing he was suggesting. Like, this can't be so. That's too simple. What are you talking about? I'm doing something wrong with my golf swing. I know I am. I must be. What's the fastest way back to California?

"Just stick with me," he said. "Can it hurt you?"

Well, no, it couldn't hurt. I mean, it wasn't as if we were doing anything really crazy here.

So I tried it. No thoughts about the golf swing. Just target and ball flight.

In Practice B, Shannon works on getting the club to the parallel (to the ground) position. New positions take time and effort before they become second nature. That's another truth amateurs must learn before they can improve.

And rhythm, tempo and balance. I started to hit the ball a little better, though my mind wasn't about to accept a modicum of success one bit. But in practice on Wednesday my game started to pick up a bit. I was actually getting my feel back to what my golf swing should feel like, the total package, and my confidence grew a tad.

Then the flag went up and it was Thursday morning. In 1976 I had finished tied for ninth at the Masters, so I knew I could play the course. But I had never gone into a major championship with my brain pestering me to get the hell out of Dodge.

It was a struggle. In heavy winds I shot "trombones" (76) in the opening round. There is nothing harder to do than swing slowly and rhythmically in wind. There is nothing that will speed up a golf swing faster than wind, I promise you, short of an electrode in your rear end. Actually, I felt I did a pretty good job in trying to keep it slow. Tempo, rhythm and balance, the man said.

Friday I teed off early. I shoot 66. Boom! What were the golf gods up to now? But "it" was there. I could feel it. It was right. The total package was there. Welcome back, "It."

I leapfrogged the field. On Saturday I played with Curtis Strange. We were among the last groups. I shot a two-under-par 70. I was tied for the lead with Ben Crenshaw after 54 holes. Crenshaw and I were paired in the final group on Sunday. I was just shaking my head, wondering if this new input from Kostis really would pull me through.

After eight holes on the front nine I had held my own. And then I drained a putt for birdie on the ninth hole to take the lead by one stroke going into, yes, The Back Nine on Sunday at the Masters.

Sports fans, all I can tell you is that there's no feeling quite like it.

---

## MALTBIE'S ALL-TIME RANGE TIPS . . .

- THINK TARGET ONLY (A), OR
- THINK SWING ONLY (B) . . .
- ONE OR THE OTHER, BUT DON'T MIX A WITH B.
- DEVELOP A PRE-SHOT ROUTINE.
- ALWAYS HAVE A PLAN.
- NO GUESSWORK, INCLUDING FROM FELLOW RANGE RATS.
- LEARN EXACT WEDGE DISTANCES.
- BUILD A STATION (ALIGNMENT, BALL POSITION).
- GOLF-SPECIFIC DRILLS ONLY.
- "WARM DOWN" BEFORE LEAVING (DRIVER, WEDGE SHOTS INTERCHANGED).

**About "building a station" — the club on the ground assists John Flanagan in lining up. Shoulders, hips, knees and feet parallel to the club on the ground.**

The back nine was pistols and shotguns at the OK Corral. There were six of us right there at the top of the leader board the whole nine holes.

I ended up losing by a shot. That was the year that Larry Mize, Seve Ballesteros and Greg Norman were in a playoff, and Mize canned that pitch shot on the 11th to win. I was one stroke out of that playoff. Was this the same head case, clueless *and* prayerless, who came tooling up to the clubhouse just a few days back?

It was the biggest lesson I had ever learned in my life about how to practice. I went into the Masters with absolutely nothing. And I felt like I worked on absolutely nothing to get my swing back. I was fascinated. What did I learn? I learned there was a way to practice getting my game from the practice tee to the golf course.

I learned there are two different, distinct ways to practice. And you had best not confuse them.

There is practicing golf, which means

One more look at a "station" drill, this one to make sure the club stays on plane throughout the swing. A section of a two-by-four will do.

practicing playing the game. And that means the focus is target and ball flight, just as when you play the game. Rhythm, tempo and balance are the watchwords. Hear me now: This is the practice to use to get your game from the range to the golf course. Usually this type of practice should be employed before a round of golf, or during a tournament.

Then there is the practice that involves the mechanics of the golf swing, which means working on a swing position or fundamentals. This is the practice to use away from the golf course, usually after a round or in preparation for a tournament. But not *during* a tournament or *before* a round.

These are two completely different types of practice sessions. Mix them up and soon you will be visited by a couple of big dudes in white coats.

To be honest, I knew absolutely nothing about how to get my game from the practice tee to the golf course before that 1987 Masters. I knew nothing about how to practice getting my game to the golf course.

The more you remove golf from the target, which is the whole point of the game, the more problems any golfer is bound to have. If you remember that point, you are not as likely to get out of whack. Now I had learned an entirely new way of practicing this game. Fascinating. So simple anyone can do it. Scratch players, 36-handicappers, women, junior golfers, seniors . . . it doesn't matter. By thinking target and using good rhythm and timing, any golfer can reset the priorities and get back to playing golf. If you are struggling with your swing and you really don't know how to fix it, with good rhythm, tempo and balance you will be surprised how the golf swing can repair itself.

If you can turn your attention strongly enough to the target, keenly enough focused on the target and how you want the ball to look going to that target, the body will tend to react and do those things necessary to make good things happen. You don't have to know why. It just does.

If you've played golf for any length of time, you've found a way to hit the ball. No matter who you are as a golfer, female or male, young or getting up there, you have found a way to hit the ball on the golf course.

Now, the general impression among golfers is they're not hitting the ball anywhere near the way they should be hitting it. But even a 20-handicapper who has played the game a while has found a way to hit the ball. It's a style. And that is important. It is something we all have. Let's call it a "thumb print."

We all have particular quirks and faults and things in our golf swing we wish were not there. We anguish over how to make them go away. But they never do, not really, and they never will, no matter what golf book you're reading. It's all part of the "thumb print." Part of my thumb print is I have a tendency to take the club back a little bit hooded. That creates a timing problem for me. But it is part of my package and I accept it.

Don't forsake your thumb print. It is who you are. Work with it. Not against it. When you have developed a style (found a way to hit the ball), for you to try to change your swing or swing like someone else is a waste of time. That is the ultimate in guesswork, and guess-

work in golf is a no-no. Guesswork is trying to throw a Band-Aid on what could be a wound that requires stitches. It is trying to find a quick-fix to get you through the moment. These fixes usually are one-round wonders, at best. Might even be one-swing wonders.

It amazes me still how even the top pros play this game of guesswork on the range. I'm certainly not immune. I have certainly done my share. Somehow at Augusta National, at the U.S. Open, at the British Open and at the PGA, there

Check out the board parallel to the club in Mike's "station" — that is what caused ski hero Franz Klammer to call the drill dangerous. And the guy likes to schuss down a mountain at 80 mph on slats. Peter Kostis and I were more than amused.

are guys beating balls out there past last call trying to find something other than who they are. Change this, change that. Guesswork from swing to swing. Absolute madness.

When you get right down to it, probably the biggest secret of golf is not knowing everything there is to know about golf, but merely knowing what it takes to operate your own game.

Bruce Lietzke, who practiced sparingly at best, is one golfer who really knows his own game. One year at the end of the season, Lietzke told his caddie that he was going home and he would not be touching his clubs for months.

Well, that caddie didn't believe for a moment that Bruce would not touch his clubs in his time off. So the caddie slipped a banana up under the club cover of Bruce's driver. Bruce came back at the start of the next season. The caddie removed the cover and, sure enough, there was this very rotten banana.

Lietzke has made it plain that he never tries anything new. That's the key to his whole game. He has always been satisfied with the way he goes about playing and practicing. Bruce has been great at practice in the sense that he merely does those things he knows he can do, and nothing more.

There are a couple of ways you can look at that. It is possible Bruce Lietzke has sold himself short. Maybe if he had worked on things, he might have been a better player. But I'm in the other camp. I say he was as good as he could be by sticking with what works best for him.

Repetition is what this game is all about. Stick with what works for you on the golf course. Let that grow. Work on that part on the range. (We will get into mechanics in short order.) Give new respect to the shots you know. Grow on that. Let that develop.

The next time you find yourself doing guesswork on the range, go back to rhythm, tempo and balance. Think target. Now don't misunderstand me — I'm not throwing this out there as a blanket cure-all. But I will tell you that I have never seen a golf swing damaged by thoughts of rhythm, timing and balance.

"RANGE RATS"

# Chapter 3

## 'PRACTICE B' FOR SWING FIXES . . .
## THE CULTURE OF THE RANGE RAT . . .
## HOGAN'S LEGACY . . .
## PLAN PRACTICES . . .

When I was 14 years old I had one of those experiences a golfer remembers the rest of his life. The U.S. Open was at the Olympic Club in San Francisco, and this San Jose boy was going up to see his first major golf championship in person.

That was the year Arnold Palmer blew a seven-stroke lead on the final nine holes to Billy Casper, losing in the playoff the next day. But the memories I have are of Ben Hogan.

The teacher who taught me the game at San Jose Country Club, Eddie Duino, had spoken of Hogan as the greatest ball striker who ever lived. So did everyone else. They talked about this man in a strange way, as if he were a saint. They all said this may be his last major championship appearance, so I went to see this man Ben Hogan. I wanted to find out what the fuss was all about.

Wow!

Hogan played a practice round with Ken Venturi, my boyhood idol, and Frank Beard. When Hogan hit the ball I saw something different from anything in golf I had ever seen before.

What I noticed, what I took with me from that day, was the consistency of his trajectory. Every iron took off on the same line. It didn't matter if it was a 7-iron or a 4-iron, they all had the same launch. It was just brilliant to watch. It never varied. It was like every shot went through the same hoop. I wondered how he did that.

They told me that Hogan was a self-made man, a self-taught man, that he got where he was by practicing more than anyone else on Tour. So I watched

**When a Tour pro practices, he likely has a practice plan.**

him practice. What I saw was a golf swing that could repeat itself. Just looking at that swing, there was a sense that somehow it worked like a machine.

It was on that day I realized that repetition is the key to this game.

Hogan was a man with whom we could all identify, because he did not consider himself a born golfer. He believed the game could be learned.

He knew he didn't have a swing like Sam Snead's, which looked as if it were a birthright. But that didn't stop Ben Hogan. His firm belief was that it was not necessarily talent that could propel a golfer to great heights. Hard work would serve just as well. He would hit golf balls until his hands bled, then soak

them in salt water. Then he would hit golf balls again. He was like a scientist looking for a universal application, a unifying force to the chaos called the golf swing.

And he found it. He called "it" fundamentals.

A secret or two might have come along the way, and I'm of the opinion Hogan took a couple of those to the grave with him. But that's not the point. Hogan was the first golfer really to deal with repetition in the golf swing. He believed that if he found the proper set of fundamentals they could be learned and practiced. There you have it, sports fans.

Ben Hogan is the Father of All

Range Rats. He *is* "da man," and thank God he didn't have to listen to that unfortunate phrase. Hogan made practice popular in golf, the man who showed us that this game could be learned if we just worked hard enough at the right things.

Before Hogan, the swing was treated as something of a mystery — it was taught through method, through secrets, through feel. Hogan took it to the next level. No more secrets. Fundamentals were the name of the game. Universal fundamentals that could be practiced.

He wrote a book in 1957 called *Five Lessons, The Modern Fundamentals of Golf*. That book is considered the bible on Tour. It was the first golf book to deal with and stress fundamentals. Nothing better has come along since.

Hogan had secrets, but he practiced fundamentals. When he had a problem with his game, he went back to his fundamentals on the range. After his book was published, The Culture of the Range Rat began to spread. By the time I got on Tour, in 1975, every Range Rat I knew had a copy of Ben's book in his car. And those fundamentals have

**Range Rats galore, happily hitting away. They even draw a small gallery.**

Dr. Carl Borders, University of Oregon player Mike Sica and Shannon Rouillard — different in many ways. But they share a love of the game and they are happy to be Range Rats.

changed more than one swing on Tour.

When Scott Simpson first came on the Tour in 1979, he had an upright swing. But when he won the U.S. Open at Olympic in 1987, that swing had been changed dramatically. And he had that same launch angle off his irons that I saw with Hogan. Simpson told the press after he won that Hogan's book turned him around. He had been practicing Hogan's fundamentals.

Simpson is not alone, he's just a prime example of how the book has changed careers. On the men's Tour, stories about the book are as legendary as Hogan himself in the Range Rat culture. Every week on the range, it seems there's another myth attributed to that book.

It was a book that had a hard beginning, I can tell you.

Herbert Warren Wind, the man who wrote it, was first turned away by Hogan. Wind visited Hogan in Texas, and Hogan was not at all impressed by the idea. He sent Wind home.

But Wind sent Hogan the drawings Anthony Ravielli had done for the book, and that changed Hogan's mind. He said he would do the book if Ravielli would work with him on improving those drawings. Wind spent two weeks at Hogan's house for the text. Four months were spent on refining Ravielli's drawings. Hogan wanted it right.

The fundamentals of the game are pretty well established these days, most right out of Hogan's book. And it is

## PRO 'RATS' MOST FUN TO PRACTICE WITH . . .

- J.C. SNEAD
- LEE TREVINO
- FUZZY ZOELLER
- MIKE REID
- ANDREW MAGEE
- JOANNE CARNER
- GARY McCORD
- CRAIG STADLER
- LARRY ZIEGLER
- CHI CHI RODRIGUEZ
- JESPER PARNEVIK
- JERRY HEARD

important to note that all these fundamentals are done pre-shot, *before* the swing starts.

Anyone can learn them. That is the beauty of fundamentals. It takes no special talent or physical ability to use them. They just enhance your own potential. But as Hogan himself dramatically demonstrated, fundamentals scream to be practiced. This is true for any golfer at any level. Period.

This practice — the one Hogan made popular — involves working on swing positions or mechanics, and that means fundamentals. It's different from the practice I learned at the 1987 Masters. That practice has absolutely nothing to do with any of the technical aspects of the golf swing. Practice A is a practice devoted to playing the game, remember? It is practice generally used before a round of golf or during a tournament. In this chapter we are talking about "Practice B."

This is where I work on technical parts of my game. And at that point, if I think my shaft position is too vertical midway through my backswing, and I want to flatten that some, this is the time I work on trying to achieve that position.

And then everything changes.

All I am trying to do is create something technical. Now I no longer grade myself on how the ball flies, the results of the shot itself. I don't care where the damn ball goes, because that's not my goal. This is Practice B, I say again.

There has to be a real differentiation between the two types of practice. If you have the sense I am repeating myself, you would be right. I can't emphasize that enough. You have to know what to expect, what to look for, from each practice session.

If I'm working on positions in the golf swing, my goal simply is to try to put the club in a position and worry about nothing else. Now I can't be concerned about golf, certainly not for awhile.

Even if I hit that ball 40 yards out of bounds, I have to look at my goal and ask the proper question — did I put the club in the proper position? If not, am I getting there? If I can look at myself

**Bill Scott "pures" a 5-iron. Now, how do you get that swing to the golf course? Olympic pro Jim Lucius knows.**

34

and say that, yes, I did, almost, then I have to be satisfied. Even if that ball was last seen curving wildly over fences, bouncing off trees, or dribbling along the ground. It matters not.

What's important is I'm creating a habit. You've got to have patience to create a healthy habit.

Hogan said it takes "21 days" on the range to create a habit or correct a bad habit. That's pretty much been proven from everything I've heard and read. If you can discipline yourself to do something the same way repeatedly, it will become habit after about three weeks. That is, if you will really, really, really work at it. Sorry, no shortcuts.

But for Pete's sake give yourself time to create this habit. Do not jump right into it before a club tournament or at a big Saturday grudge match, or you will be quickly confusing the two different types of practice. At the 1998 U.S. Open at Olympic, there was a perfect example of what can happen. Tiger Woods was working with his instructor, Butch Harmon, on creating a specific position in his backswing. And Tiger worked on that position in practice right through the tournament.

Woods was closing the clubface a little in his takeaway. Harmon wanted him to open the clubface more in his backswing. There was a specific position Harmon gave Woods. He wanted the toe of the club pointing right up to the sky when the swing reached his hips. He wanted the club to be in that specific position, and that's how Woods prac-

ticed — he would stop at his hips and check his position.

This position was somewhat new to Woods, and he had problems. On the range, Woods would try to get back into ball flight and target, but he would always stop here and there to check that position in his backswing. He had created the classic confusion in the two different types of practice. He mixed them up, creating conflict. He struggled

The stone marks the yardage to five target greens. Learning the distances you get from each of your clubs — especially wedges — is essential to better golf scores. Trust me.

to make the cut and never seriously contended for the title.

Woods was going through the growing pains of learning a position in the golf swing. I would suggest to him never do that again the week of a major.

By the time the British Open came around, Tiger had practiced that position for more than 21 days. He had created the habit. And he was right in the hunt, losing by a single stroke at Royal Birkdale.

When you work on a position, it throws all your rhythm and timing off because you're doing something you're not used to be doing. The trap for most golfers in this type of practice is to start thinking, "Oh, this isn't doing me any good." And then try something different. Before you know it, that golfer is doing, yes, guesswork.

But if you stick with the fundamental you are working on and dedicate yourself to it for awhile, I promise you that you will get better. You will improve. The new move or position will eventually integrate itself with the rhythm and tempo of your swing.

Of course, with the talent we have on Tour, there are the exceptions. Some have a special talent and they don't have to wade through those 21 days. Fred Couples comes to mind, and I don't know how he does it. I've seen him work on a new position with his teacher, Paul Marchand. The next day he shoots 66. Hello, golf! That's a rare talent. Most of us are like a Hogan, blue-collar kinds of golfers who have to work our buns off to improve.

I remember once a bunch of us were Range Ratting, and we were all talking about who was the greatest golfer of all time. Of course somebody said, "Ben Hogan struck the ball better than anybody." Well, Dave Hill popped in and said, "Oh, yeah? Well, if Hogan was so good how come he had to practice eight hours a day? Give me Jack Nicklaus, who beats everybody in his spare time."

We owe Hogan for teaching us that repetition is the single most necessary ingredient to play this game at a high level, or any level, and for teaching us that repetition comes through practice. But we owe Jack Nicklaus for showing us *how* to practice. It took us about a decade to catch on, but nobody ever said golfers were always the brightest guys on the planet.

I never knew Nicklaus to practice for any great periods of time. The duration of his practice session may have been shorter than those for most of us, but that didn't seem to matter. I always had the sense that Nicklaus accomplished exactly what he wanted to accomplish every time he went out to the range.

Nicklaus was always very orderly and disciplined, legendary Nicklaus traits, and that carried over to his practice sessions. Jack would always come to the driving range with a specific idea of what he wanted to accomplish in that practice session. He had a specific idea of where he thought his golf swing might be deficient — or where a bad habit had somehow been created — and a specific idea of what to do about it. He would use that swing thought, and nothing else.

After a few swings, if it became apparent to Jack that he was wrong, he left. *He left*, mind you!

Jack Nicklaus never played guesswork. He did not stick around playing head games if he was wrong about the solution he took to the range. The lesson we all learned from Nicklaus is not to go to the range before thinking it out first. That way the mind is clear. Look specifically at what you're trying to address, with the specific way you will go about accomplishing it, and practice becomes much easier. My suggestion to anyone is to look at the part of your swing that is failing and come up with a workable solution before machine-gun-

ning balls into oblivion. Set a plan. Chart a plan for yourself before you go to the range. Stick with your objectives.

I dare you to follow a concrete plan and not improve. It should be a plan you've developed in conjunction with a professional, with some professional advice. Devising a plan, implementing the plan, and sticking to the plan will work. Anything else is, yes, guesswork.

For example, let's say we've figured out that the real problem was that the ball was constantly going left of target. Well, let's see. That must mean the swing was getting out of plane somewhere, or the clubface was closed at impact. The easiest plan of action would be to check alignment, to make sure the feet or shoulders are not aimed too far right. That would certainly throw the swing plane off kilter.

---

## PERFECT PRACTICE IS . . .

- NOT HOW MANY BALLS YOU HIT, BUT THE QUALITY OF PRACTICE.
- GOING TO THE RANGE WITH A PLAN.
- ALLOWING 21 DAYS OF WORK FOR A NEW SWING POSITION TO BECOME A HABIT.
- PAYING NO ATTENTION TO BALL FLIGHT WHEN LEARNING A NEW SWING POSITION.
- CONCENTRATING ON TARGET, NOT SWING POSITIONS, BEFORE PLAYING.
- NEVER, NEVER MIXING PRACTICING GOLF WITH PRACTICING TECHNIQUE.
- KNOWING YOUR DISTANCES.
- AVOIDING GUESSWORK.
- THINKING FUNDAMENTALS FIRST.
- HITTING AT A TARGET.
- KNOWING YOUR STATS.

This example by Shannon is what I call Practice A. She's thinking only target, balance and tempo . . .

So now you go to the range, and you ask someone to take a look at your alignment. Ask where your shoulders are pointing. Put a club down by your feet and see if your feet are aligned toward the target. If your friend tells you your alignment is a joke, now you've got a job in front of you. But if that's not the problem, stop. Get away for a moment. Devise another plan.

As long as you have a clear idea of what you are trying to accomplish when you are striking shots, and as long as you have a clear objective for the specific the type of practice you're doing, then your practice time is positive.

The most effective way for someone to get better in this game is to deal with and try to duplicate your swing each and every shot, each and every day. Grip. Stance. Alignment. Ball position. Those are the great fundamentals of the game, and with the possible exception of a physical deformity, there's no reason Jack Nicklaus or myself or David Duval or Tiger Woods can do them any better than the next guy. These fundamentals take work, but they are all done before the ball leaves the club. Think about that for a minute.

We all learned how to grip the club. It felt strange for awhile. But then it became habit. I don't think I've had a conscious thought about my grip in 30 years. Learning it was not easy. It becomes a habit. But it is necessary to put in the time to get to that point. You are training yourself to put your hands on the club in a proper way.

When a Tour pro goes to the range after his round to work on some technical swing problem, usually the first thing he will do is ask someone to check his alignment. He will ask a friend to stand behind him and ask him where he is aiming. Feet. Shoulders. Hip. Knees. The basics.

Often, we build ourselves a "station." Go to any PGA Tour event — men's women, seniors — and head on out to the range. You will see more than one pro with a couple of clubs on the ground, one along his target line and the other perpendicular to that club, intersecting the ball with his left heel. That's called building a station, and you should do it.

When you go to the practice tee to work on something technical, put a club down on the ground first for alignment. The club should point to your target. Now put another club down across the first club, at a right angle, from the ball to your left heel. Is it on your left heel? Is it two inches inside your left heel? Four inches inside your left heel? Where is it? Take note.

Now you have built yourself a station. But do it the same way every time. That is key. Once you're there, and you know where your spots are, then you can always go back and check. Am I in the same spots? Am I the same distance from the ball? Am I farther from the ball? Well, that will certainly change

the swing plan. And certainly change your swing shape.

Repetition is just so damn important, as I keep saying. But there's little or no chance for repetition if you don't know your starting point. If you want to work on a specific position during the swing, it's best you get some outside help first.

Let's talk about that.

I have never really cared for instructors who teach methods. Instructors who are willing to work with your wishes, your body type, your body size, your abilities — those are the instructors I think are far more likely to show you something that will stick.

David Leadbetter or Jimmy Ballard, these are instructors who in some way have been considered method teachers. Certainly they have produced some terrific golfers. I'm not denying that. But they have a specific agenda when it comes to swinging a golf club, and it may not be your agenda. You might be taking a long trip down a blind alley.

A teacher like Leadbetter is a very technical kind of teacher. You must hit certain positions in the golf swing, and there are many of them. Not everyone can make the turn that Nick Faldo can make, or Nick Price, or Ernie Els, or Tiger Woods. My father, Lin Maltbie, is in his 70s. I can't teach him to swing a club like Nick Faldo. It's not going to happen. So find a teacher that will work with you through your personal set of characteristics, your style, your thumb print.

Working on positions in the golf

swing is simply breaking down every part of the swing. I have always thought that everything in the golf swing relates to only two things — I want the clubhead traveling with the face square, and I want the club going through impact on a line that is parallel to my feet, knees, hips and shoulders at address. All I am trying to accomplish is a square clubface and path.

If I can do that, I can play golf. So can you.

When I played for San Jose State we really didn't have a practice facility. There was a huge field down by the Municipal Stadium where the San Jose Bees played minor league baseball. It was called South Campus, and that's where we'd hit practice balls.

But across 11th Street there was a practice football field. There were those hash marks that went right up the center of the field. I would stand right between those hash marks. A goal post was at the other end of the field. I would practice striking balls right down that line between the hash

marks and through the goal post at the other end.

Talk about being able to align yourself perfectly! That was a beautiful place to practice. Setting a club down on the ground is one thing, but imagine having a chalk line running up and down the field. I was able to practice perfect alignment.

We all owe Ben Hogan for making practice popular, and Jack Nicklaus for teaching us how to practice. Okay, to add value to this book and to contribute to Range Rat lore, I am revealing a little Roger Maltbie practice secret. Hang with me now. When I am practicing swing mechanics, which usually involves hitting a lot of balls, it is necessary for me to close down the session on a positive note. No matter what I was working on, when I'm finished, I try to slow it all down before I leave the range. I grab that wedge, get back that lazy feeling, get back the tempo again before I leave. I want to warm down just as I warmed up. That way I leave the range with my tempo intact. Yesssssssss!

# Chapter 4

## A TECHNICAL JUNGLE OUT THERE . . .
## TRUTH IN NUMBERS . . .
## THE MIND WORKS BEST WITH FACTS . . .
## CHARTS GALORE . . .

When I was a kid I played and practiced at San Jose Country Club in California, long before the place got to be known as Silicon Valley. We didn't have a driving range, so I'd just go out late at night with about six balls and play all six all the way into the cup.

There were specific areas on the golf course where you could hit your own balls for practice, and there were some pretty big trees. I'd either aim at specific areas on a tree, or try to hit between them as if it were a field goal.

My teacher was the head pro, Eddie Duino, who was also the golf coach at San Jose State. Ken Venturi was on Eddie's team, so I was raised on Venturi stories. When I would want to give up practice and say my hands were sore or I

just didn't want to do it anymore, Eddie would start a story.

He would point to a tree and say that Venturi would stand here until he could knock every leaf off that tree with a 4-iron. Sometimes it took him all day, but he would get every leaf. So I hit a ton of balls.

When I started playing the Tour with my first sponsor I didn't even have a credit card, just went around on cash. I drove an old Ford Galaxy 500 that was an ugly yellow color. I shouldn't say that, really, because it was my parents' car at one time, and I really was grateful. But that's how I cruised the Tour. They just handed you a road map back then, not much more.

Nobody ever had a teaching pro out on Tour when I started in 1975. You had to go home to see your teacher. I can remember more than once being lost with my game, flying from the East

Coast out to California to see my teacher for a day, and then flying back.

Many of the courses I played back then didn't even have a driving range, like the course I grew up on. Practice facilities were not considered a priority. They are a relatively new addition.

Today there is much more care given to creating and maintaining practice facilities at a golf course. But not the older courses. With a lot of these old golf courses, it is a problem when you try to hold a major championship like a U.S. Open.

Look at Winged Foot, a perfect example. You've got to go practice on the East course. There is no driving range. There is a little field where you can hit shots, but there are only maybe 20 stalls and that's about it. So they have to use another golf course.

And look at Augusta National. For all Augusta National offers, they have just two little strips either side of Magnolia Lane with a huge net at the end to keep the golf balls from crossing Washington Avenue.

Today, the practice facilities are elaborate, and so are the people you find there. Now when you go to the range at any Tour tournament, the tee area is lined with male and female coaches and instructors. Hands-on people.

Plus, nearby you will find videotape equipment, fitness trailers and golf-club reps who will repair or alter your sticks. We used to have to change our own grips back at the hotel or ship the clubs

What? No woods on this range? Is this somebody's idea of a joke?

out, maybe find a local guy who could do it, if you could trust him. I did my own. Now all Tour players can get their clubs fixed on the spot by the manufacturer. They can get a quick check on their swings by their own instructors. If the instructor's not around, you can take a videotape of your swing, FedEx it out and have it back in two days with your instructor's comments.

It's a technical jungle on the range these days — psychologists, nutritionists, therapists, personal trainers. Suddenly everybody has an entourage, like a rock star.

When Tiger Woods came out on Tour, he didn't just come out with his instructor, Butch Harmon. He came out with Team Tiger. And that team had been together awhile. Times have changed. A minor understatement. Today, teaching golf is far more technical — biomechanics and anatomical positions, computers, video and the like. This is the real world now. Nothing is left to chance.

And part of all that is keeping stats — charting out a round.

Jack Nicklaus generally is considered to be the first person to chart the game. Ben Hogan didn't do that. For all of Hogan's technical expertise, it never carried over to the golf course. For Hogan, it all was done with the eyes. Eyes easily can be tricked. Hogan believed in "feel" out there on the course, not numbers.

But Jack has always believed in cold, hard numbers. He has created an inter-

## 10 TOUR PLAYERS WHO GET THE MOST OUT OF PRACTICE . . .

- JACK NICKLAUS
- TOM KITE
- NICK PRICE
- BOB ESTES
- DAVIS LOVE III
- DAVID DUVAL
- BRUCE LIETZKE
- VIJAY SINGH
- JUSTIN LEONARD
- LEE TREVINO

esting argument — did Jack win all those major championships and beat everybody's brains in because he was better physically, or was he just better prepared and tougher mentally? He never went to the practice tee without a definite idea of what he wanted to accomplish. He never played a tournament without thoroughly charting out the course. No detail was left out for the four majors.

Jack was uncanny in his ability to look at a golf course, size it up and make a game plan. One thing he did that always blew me away was pick the winning score in a major with astonishing accuracy.

I was paired with Nicklaus in 1975 at Firestone Country Club when he won the PGA Championship. Some of you may remember that famous Sunday 8-iron from 200 yards on the 16th hole,

43

over the trees and the pond in front. I certainly remember it.

I had never played a golf course set up for a major championship before, where the greens are all waxed up, firm and hard, and the rough is up, the fairways narrowed. It was a long, punishing par-70 golf course — the toughest I had ever seen.

In the first round, Ed Dougherty and Bob Wynn both were shooting lights out. Dougherty was 6-under par in the first round. I saw his name on the board, and I said to Jack, "Geez, can you believe he's 6-under through 13?" Jack gave me that hard look of his and replied, "It doesn't make any difference — 275 will win this championship.'"

Uh, okay. What did Jack shoot? He shot 275. Did he win? Can fish swim?

Nicklaus would go to the site of a major championship the week before and pace off distances and get to know the shots he would have to play. Then he would go home and work on those shots and come back to the site on Tuesday. Never before Tuesday.

He also charted out his game during a major. He kept his stats. After each round. He knew how many greens he hit in regulation, how many fairways he hit, how many putts, and so forth. He would work that out before he went to the practice tee after each round. He knew what he had to work on to prepare for the next day.

Hard, cold numbers. You simply cannot argue with hard, cold numbers. Why? Because perception and reality

are two different beasts. You may think there is a glitch in your swing, and that was the reason you shot that humiliating 79. But the numbers may tell you something stunningly different.

Check the numbers and you may find that you hit enough greens in regulation, but that your putting absolutely sucked. If you hit 12 greens, and that's your average, fine. But if you had 38 putts, that is a problem, or you had better find some other line of work. That's about eight strokes above where you should be if you want to win on Tour.

Better not be on the range working out a glitch that didn't feel right. Better be on the putting green. The evidence is in. You just can't argue with numbers.

Most of us on Tour never took the time to chart out our rounds after we played. That's just one more reason Nicklaus always beat everyone silly. He wanted it more, and those course charts and post-round stats he recorded certainly gave him another advantage. A huge advantage, if you ask me.

The Tour has since acknowledged the value of a player's knowing his stats. The Tour also figured correctly the public might be interested as well. So the Tour started keeping stat sheets for us around the mid-1980s. Those stats amount to a great tool.

The stats on Tour have since been adjusted and modified to make them even more salient. In fact, they have become a sidebar competition in themselves. The players with the best stats are given awards at the end of the year.

It is easy to see why player Mike Sica hits the ball a ton — he's coiled to kill it. The beautiful range at San Francisco's Olympic Club is among the very best.

You get a trophy for being the best putter, the best in sand saves, hitting greens in regulation, and so forth.

I am absolutely amazed we still have players on Tour who don't know how to use those stats. They'll finish their rounds with, say, 35 putts, and where do they go at the end of the day? To the practice tee! Not to the putting green. That doesn't make sense to me. Why don't you go over to the putting green? Hello? Anybody home?

But some players — at all levels, both genders — simply have to go hit balls after a disappointing round. Sometimes it is almost as if it were some sort of penance. Or they go to the range out of sheer fascination with hitting golf balls. To be honest, I always kind of felt that way myself. It's a Range Rat thing.

A fault of mine was I got a bigger kick at watching a golf ball fly. I got a bigger kick out of controlling the golf ball, its trajectories and curving. For me, there was no feeling like hitting a flush 3-iron just the way you wanted to hit it. That gave me my jollies.

Grinding away on a putting green never thrilled me. I didn't get the same feedback from it as I got from spending hours on the range. The point is, if the stats tell you that's what you've got to

Practicing with a Range Rat companion who can check your alignment or spot flaws works with Practice B. I suggest also that you see a good local teacher who will teach within your "style."

do, then that's what you've got to do. No matter where you get your jollies.

But it is not for me to tell you why you should love golf. It's not for me to tell you what part of the game you should love most. It is for me to tell you that if you want to improve your game, there are ways to do it — practical, procedural, objective ways to become a better golfer.

With those stat sheets, now we know what to practice after a round. It gives the player something concrete. Regardless of what you may think you have to do after a round, the charts tell you what you have to do. And certainly for the average player, his or her improvement can be dramatic because there's so much more margin for improvement.

That is why I have included charts in this book. Keep your own stats. Then you will know what to work on when you go practice. Check your stats after one round, or take much stronger statistical samples of your game by measuring your play after five rounds or 10. Even 20. If you are diligent, you are going to be amazed at what you find, especially if all the rounds are on your home course.

At this point I should say that keeping good charts and stats depends on your ability to remember all your shots. If you are concentrating, focused, you will remember them all — the club you hit, the distance and where the ball ended up. If not, you won't. No self-respecting Range Rat could fail to remember every shot in the round, right?

That said, I also strongly suggest that if you really want to improve, you should chart where your misses go on the course during a round. Stats are an invaluable aid to practice. That's just the bottom line. To my knowledge, these Tour charts have never been made available to the general public. So, with this book, here is your chance to chart your own game, keep your own stats.

You can use these charts in a general sense, or you can be as specific as you wish. Personally, I don't think the charts, or stats sheets, on Tour are detailed enough. They don't tell me enough.

Here is what I mean: In 1998, Tiger Woods finished 147th in putting, but he also finished the year as the No. 1 player in the world. What does that tell you? Does it tell you that he had better go find a putting green and pitch a tent?

Not necessarily. A guy like Woods, who hits a lot of greens in regulation, is going to have many two-putt greens for par. A guy who misses a lot of greens is going to have a lot of one-putts for par. So, you have to compare the stats to find out really what they're saying. If you hit a lot of greens, your putting stats will be higher.

There's another reason I don't think the stats sheets on Tour are specific enough. These questions are never addressed: How many times were you short of your target with an iron to a green? Or long? How many times were you right or left of the tee? That would paint a better picture than the fact that you just (a) hit the fairway, or (b) missed the fairway. Or (a) hit the green or (b) missed the green.

I have hit some pretty doggone good tee shots that have missed the fairway maybe by three inches in the short fringe off the fairway. And I was pleased with that tee shot. But it counts as a miss on the stats sheet. The wild hook or slice that went out of bounds or into the jungle, that had a far more devastating effect on my score. The stats we use on Tour will never reflect that.

Take a bunker stat. A sand-saving stat may not be a measure of your sand shot as it is as a measure of how well you putt. If it is a sand-save on the stat sheet, you may have hit a terrible bunker shot to 30 feet, but holed the putt. It counts the same as if you hit a bunker shot to an inch from the cup and tapped it in.

---

## PERFECT PRACTICE IS NOT . . .

- SKIPPING WARMUPS.
- TRYING THIS AND THAT.
- MACHINE-GUNNING IT OUT THERE.
- FORGETTING TO BRING A PLAN.
- HITTING RANDOMLY.
- MIXING PRACTICE A AND PRACTICE B.
- SNUBBING THE SHORT GAME.
- SHOWING OFF.
- GETTING ANGRY.

So even the stats can be misleading. And that is why I have included a place on the charts in this book to make notes. It's a box for your comment, for more detail. Jot down what really happened with that sand save. Make a note of whether it was a missed putt or a missed bunker shot. Perhaps make up your own code or short-hand. Mark down a missed fairway, but jot down in the comment box that it was a super drive on the fringe, or that the ball went into the jungle left or right. Mark down a missed green, but comment on whether it was short, left, right or long. Maybe it was on the fringe. Or maybe it hit the pond in front of the green.

You can break the stats up into a series of small pictures, or you can look at them in the greater picture. Say I'm a 12-handicapper. I may not be the greatest driver in the world, but as I look at the whole picture, I really fall off in short-game play. Now we know the greatest need for concern. We know where to work harder. If you *really* want to improve.

But if you know that "I really suck at bunker play" or "I really stink inside of 50 yards," now you've got a pretty good barometer on how you can most efficiently go about improving your game and lowering your scores. Not just get a little better, but a *lot* better. The bottom line is, charts will promote understanding and eliminate guesswork. And managing your game will become easier. It is akin to running a business — you have to take inventory. This is it.

Looking at it another way, the charts will show you your "fail points." Where is *your* fail point? No matter what you think your fail point is, where is your fail point in reality? Where do you most commonly fail? The charts will tell you. Then you can come up with a plan to kick that fail-point habit.

Also, it is a good idea to bring your golf professional into the loop. The results of your new charts will make his or her job a hell of a lot easier, I would wager.

# The C

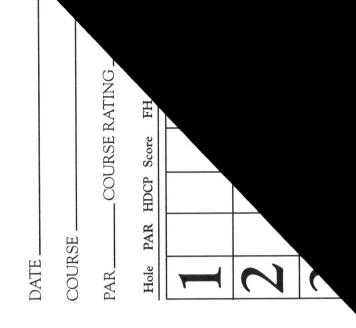

DATE

COURSE

PAR ——— COURSE RATING

PAR   HDCP   Score   FH

Hole   PAR   HDCP   Score   FH

1
2

T he charts on the ensuing pages absolutely essential to your making yourself a better golfer. That is true for scratch players and high-handicappers, both genders and any i These charts are similar to the charts supplied for on Tour to help them audit their games. The public r gets to see those, so you are now in on the secret. I ha added a few categories that should be helpful to playe all levels, plus a place to make notes.

If you are sincerely interested in playing more satisf golf, sorry, no matter what anyone tells you to the con trary, there are no shortcuts, no quick fixes. There is c one guaranteed way to get better — practice. And the more practice.

So, how to use these charts:

• Start by keeping an accurate scorecard for each round you play. If you can't remember the shots you h on each hole, make mental notes. Or even take a little notebook with you. I say again, if you really are committed to improving, this will do it for you.

• Then back home after the round, fill in the charts, front nine and back nine, hole by hole.

• Using your scorecard, fill in the spaces for par on each hole, plus the handicap ratings so that you will be able to measure how you played the hard holes and the easier holes over the span of, say, 10 rounds.

• Count the number of Fairways Hit (FH) on your tee shots (except par-3s), and note where you missed the fairway, if you did. Examples: Trees left. Right bunker. Short rough right. Deep rough left. Topped. Duck hook. Pop-up.

• GIR means Greens In Regulation, the number of shots it takes to reach the green. "Regulation" is par less two putts, so on a par-5, you have three shots to get "home" in regulation.

• UD means Up and Down, making par or better when you miss the green in regulation. Say you just missed the green in two. You chip onto the green and make a putt. You got the ball "up" onto the green and "down." into the hole. You may want to note this in the "Comments" box on the chart.

• Sand Saves is similar to Up and Down. You missed the green, landed in a bunker and then got it up and down to save par. For the purposes of this book, let's also count Sand Saves for bogeys, but nothing higher. Don't forget to make a pertinent note.

• In the Comments boxes, be sure to note penalty strokes such as Out of Bounds (OB) and Lost Ball (LB). Hazard Penalties (HP) is for ponds and streams.

• Lay Up (LU) indicates those times you may have to lay up short of the green because of the length of a hole, or to avoid a hazard. It may indicate you played the hole as well as you can, even though you were over par on the hole.

• Be sure to note the weather. Obviously, weather-related conditions — wind, soft greens, hard fairways, etc. — will affect scores greatly.

• At the top of each back-nine chart are two sections to keep track of your practice sessions. Remember, it is vitally important — if you really, really want to improve — to have a plan that you take to the range. Plan A or Plan B.

This will take patience if you tend to the details and give the charts your very best efforts. The mere focus alone will improve your game, as will the pre-shot routine which you must practice also — and that means you low-handicappers, too.

We also have included a copy of the chart in the back of the book which you can tear out and photocopy.

To my knowledge there never has been a golf book totally dedicated to practice. Specifically, how to practice. And beyond that, having fun doing it. Become a Range Rat, if you are not one already. We are a special breed.

WEATHER _____

_____ BACK TEES _____ REGULAR _____ LADIES_____

_____ WINTER RULES _____ SUMMER RULES _____

| | GIR | UD | SS | Putts | Comments |
|---|---|---|---|---|---|
| 3 | | | | | |
| 4 | | | | | |
| 5 | | | | | |
| 6 | | | | | |
| 7 | | | | | |
| 8 | | | | | |
| 9 | | | | | |
| TOTAL | | | | | |

HDCP — Scorecard Handicap Rating    UD — Up & Down    LB— Lost Ball
FH — Fairways Hit    SS — Sand Saves    HP— Hazard Penalties
GIR — Greens In Regulation    OB — Out of Bounds    LU— Lay up

PRACTICE SITE _____ | PRACTICE SITE _____

PRACTICE TYPE (A or B) _____ | PRACTICE TYPE (A or B) _____

NO. OF BALLS HIT _____ | NO. OF BALLS HIT _____

SHORT GAME | SHORT GAME

WEDGES ___ CHIPPING ___ PUTTING ___ | WEDGES ___ CHIPPING ___ PUTTING ___

| Hole | PAR | HDCP | Score | FH | GIR | UD | SS | Putts | Comments |
|------|-----|------|-------|----|----|----|----|----|----------|
| 10 | | | | | | | | | |
| 11 | | | | | | | | | |
| 12 | | | | | | | | | |
| 13 | | | | | | | | | |
| 14 | | | | | | | | | |
| 15 | | | | | | | | | |
| 16 | | | | | | | | | |
| 17 | | | | | | | | | |
| 18 | | | | | | | | | |
| TOTAL | | | | | | | | | |
| ROUND | | | | | | | | | |

**Summary/Practice Plan:**

DATE _____ WEATHER _____

COURSE _____ BACK TEES _____ REGULAR _____ LADIES_____

PAR _____ COURSE RATING _____ WINTER RULES _____ SUMMER RULES _____

| Hole | PAR | HDCP | Score | FH | GIR | UD | SS | Putts | Comments |
|---|---|---|---|---|---|---|---|---|---|
| 1 | | | | | | | | | |
| 2 | | | | | | | | | |
| 3 | | | | | | | | | |
| 4 | | | | | | | | | |
| 5 | | | | | | | | | |
| 6 | | | | | | | | | |
| 7 | | | | | | | | | |
| 8 | | | | | | | | | |
| 9 | | | | | | | | | |
| TOTAL | | | | | | | | | |

HDCP — Scorecard Handicap Rating     UD — Up & Down     LB— Lost Ball
FH — Fairways Hit     SS — Sand Saves     HP— Hazard Penalties
GIR — Greens In Regulation     OB — Out of Bounds     LU— Lay up

PRACTICE SITE _____    PRACTICE SITE _____

PRACTICE TYPE (A or B) _____    PRACTICE TYPE (A or B) _____

NO. OF BALLS HIT_____    NO. OF BALLS HIT_____

SHORT GAME                          SHORT GAME

WEDGES ___ CHIPPING ___ PUTTING ___    WEDGES ___ CHIPPING ___ PUTTING ___

| Hole | PAR | HDCP | Score | FH | GIR | UD | SS | Putts | Comments |
|------|-----|------|-------|-----|-----|-----|-----|-------|----------|
| 10 | | | | | | | | | |
| 11 | | | | | | | | | |
| 12 | | | | | | | | | |
| 13 | | | | | | | | | |
| 14 | | | | | | | | | |
| 15 | | | | | | | | | |
| 16 | | | | | | | | | |
| 17 | | | | | | | | | |
| 18 | | | | | | | | | |
| TOTAL | | | | | | | | | |
| ROUND | | | | | | | | | |

**Summary/Practice Plan:**

DATE _____ WEATHER _____

COURSE _____ BACK TEES _____ REGULAR _____ LADIES _____

PAR _____ COURSE RATING _____ WINTER RULES _____ SUMMER RULES _____

| Hole | PAR | HDCP | Score | FH | GIR | UD | SS | Putts | Comments |
|------|-----|------|-------|-----|-----|-----|-----|-------|----------|
| 1 | | | | | | | | | |
| 2 | | | | | | | | | |
| 3 | | | | | | | | | |
| 4 | | | | | | | | | |
| 5 | | | | | | | | | |
| 6 | | | | | | | | | |
| 7 | | | | | | | | | |
| 8 | | | | | | | | | |
| 9 | | | | | | | | | |
| TOTAL | | | | | | | | | |

HDCP — Scorecard Handicap Rating     UD — Up & Down     LB— Lost Ball
FH — Fairways Hit     SS — Sand Saves     HP— Hazard Penalties
GIR — Greens In Regulation     OB — Out of Bounds     LU— Lay up

| Hole | PAR | HDCP | Score | FH | GIR | UD | SS | Putts | Comments |
|------|-----|------|-------|----|----|----|----|-------|----------|
| 10 | | | | | | | | | |
| 11 | | | | | | | | | |
| 12 | | | | | | | | | |
| 13 | | | | | | | | | |
| 14 | | | | | | | | | |
| 15 | | | | | | | | | |
| 16 | | | | | | | | | |
| 17 | | | | | | | | | |
| 18 | | | | | | | | | |
| TOTAL | | | | | | | | | |
| ROUND | | | | | | | | | |

**Summary/Practice Plan:**

DATE _____ WEATHER _____

COURSE _____ BACK TEES _____ REGULAR _____ LADIES_____

PAR_____ COURSE RATING _____ WINTER RULES _____ SUMMER RULES _____

| Hole | PAR | HDCP | Score | FH | GIR | UD | SS | Putts | Comments |
|------|-----|------|-------|----|----|----|----|-------|----------|
| 1 | | | | | | | | | |
| 2 | | | | | | | | | |
| 3 | | | | | | | | | |
| 4 | | | | | | | | | |
| 5 | | | | | | | | | |
| 6 | | | | | | | | | |
| 7 | | | | | | | | | |
| 8 | | | | | | | | | |
| 9 | | | | | | | | | |
| TOTAL | | | | | | | | | |

HDCP — Scorecard Handicap Rating      UD — Up & Down          LB— Lost Ball
FH — Fairways Hit                     SS — Sand Saves         HP— Hazard Penalties
GIR — Greens In Regulation            OB — Out of Bounds      LU— Lay up

PRACTICE SITE ———————————  PRACTICE SITE ———————————

PRACTICE TYPE (A or B) —————  PRACTICE TYPE (A or B) —————

NO. OF BALLS HIT———————  NO. OF BALLS HIT———————

SHORT GAME  SHORT GAME

WEDGES ___ CHIPPING ____ PUTTING ____  WEDGES ___ CHIPPING ____ PUTTING ____

| Hole | PAR | HDCP | Score | FH | GIR | UD | SS | Putts | Comments |
|---|---|---|---|---|---|---|---|---|---|
| 10 | | | | | | | | | |
| 11 | | | | | | | | | |
| 12 | | | | | | | | | |
| 13 | | | | | | | | | |
| 14 | | | | | | | | | |
| 15 | | | | | | | | | |
| 16 | | | | | | | | | |
| 17 | | | | | | | | | |
| 18 | | | | | | | | | |
| TOTAL | | | | | | | | | |
| ROUND | | | | | | | | | |

**Summary/Practice Plan:**

DATE _____ WEATHER _____

COURSE _____ BACK TEES _____ REGULAR _____ LADIES_____

PAR_____ COURSE RATING _____ WINTER RULES _____ SUMMER RULES _____

| Hole | PAR | HDCP | Score | FH | GIR | UD | SS | Putts | Comments |
|---|---|---|---|---|---|---|---|---|---|
| 1 | | | | | | | | | |
| 2 | | | | | | | | | |
| 3 | | | | | | | | | |
| 4 | | | | | | | | | |
| 5 | | | | | | | | | |
| 6 | | | | | | | | | |
| 7 | | | | | | | | | |
| 8 | | | | | | | | | |
| 9 | | | | | | | | | |
| TOTAL | | | | | | | | | |

HDCP — Scorecard Handicap Rating UD — Up & Down LB— Lost Ball
FH — Fairways Hit SS — Sand Saves HP— Hazard Penalties
GIR — Greens In Regulation OB — Out of Bounds LU— Lay up

PRACTICE SITE _____  PRACTICE SITE _____

PRACTICE TYPE (A or B) _____  PRACTICE TYPE (A or B) _____

NO. OF BALLS HIT_____  NO. OF BALLS HIT_____

SHORT GAME  SHORT GAME

WEDGES ___ CHIPPING ___ PUTTING ___  WEDGES ___ CHIPPING ___ PUTTING ___

| Hole | PAR | HDCP | Score | FH | GIR | UD | SS | Putts | Comments |
|------|-----|------|-------|----|----|----|----|-------|----------|
| 10 | | | | | | | | | |
| 11 | | | | | | | | | |
| 12 | | | | | | | | | |
| 13 | | | | | | | | | |
| 14 | | | | | | | | | |
| 15 | | | | | | | | | |
| 16 | | | | | | | | | |
| 17 | | | | | | | | | |
| 18 | | | | | | | | | |
| TOTAL | | | | | | | | | |
| ROUND | | | | | | | | | |

Summary/Practice Plan:

DATE _____ WEATHER _____

COURSE _____ BACK TEES _____ REGULAR _____ LADIES_____

PAR_____ COURSE RATING _____ WINTER RULES _____ SUMMER RULES _____

| Hole | PAR | HDCP | Score | FH | GIR | UD | SS | Putts | Comments |
|---|---|---|---|---|---|---|---|---|---|
| 1 | | | | | | | | | |
| 2 | | | | | | | | | |
| 3 | | | | | | | | | |
| 4 | | | | | | | | | |
| 5 | | | | | | | | | |
| 6 | | | | | | | | | |
| 7 | | | | | | | | | |
| 8 | | | | | | | | | |
| 9 | | | | | | | | | |
| TOTAL | | | | | | | | | |

HDCP — Scorecard Handicap Rating    UD — Up & Down    LB— Lost Ball
FH — Fairways Hit    SS — Sand Saves    HP— Hazard Penalties
GIR — Greens In Regulation    OB — Out of Bounds    LU— Lay up

| Hole | PAR | HDCP | Score | FH | GIR | UD | SS | Putts | Comments |
|---|---|---|---|---|---|---|---|---|---|
| 10 | | | | | | | | | |
| 11 | | | | | | | | | |
| 12 | | | | | | | | | |
| 13 | | | | | | | | | |
| 14 | | | | | | | | | |
| 15 | | | | | | | | | |
| 16 | | | | | | | | | |
| 17 | | | | | | | | | |
| 18 | | | | | | | | | |
| TOTAL | | | | | | | | | |
| ROUND | | | | | | | | | |

**Summary/Practice Plan:**

DATE _____ WEATHER _____

COURSE _____ BACK TEES _____ REGULAR _____ LADIES_____

PAR_____ COURSE RATING _____ WINTER RULES _____ SUMMER RULES _____

| Hole | PAR | HDCP | Score | FH | GIR | UD | SS | Putts | Comments |
|------|-----|------|-------|----|----|----|----|-------|----------|
| 1 | | | | | | | | | |
| 2 | | | | | | | | | |
| 3 | | | | | | | | | |
| 4 | | | | | | | | | |
| 5 | | | | | | | | | |
| 6 | | | | | | | | | |
| 7 | | | | | | | | | |
| 8 | | | | | | | | | |
| 9 | | | | | | | | | |
| TOTAL | | | | | | | | | |

HDCP — Scorecard Handicap Rating    UD — Up & Down    LB— Lost Ball
FH — Fairways Hit    SS — Sand Saves    HP— Hazard Penalties
GIR — Greens In Regulation    OB — Out of Bounds    LU— Lay up

PRACTICE SITE _____  |  PRACTICE SITE _____

PRACTICE TYPE (A or B) _____  |  PRACTICE TYPE (A or B) _____

NO. OF BALLS HIT_____  |  NO. OF BALLS HIT_____

SHORT GAME  |  SHORT GAME

WEDGES ___ CHIPPING ___ PUTTING ___  |  WEDGES ___ CHIPPING ___ PUTTING ___

| Hole | PAR | HDCP | Score | FH | GIR | UD | SS | Putts | Comments |
|------|-----|------|-------|----|----|----|----|-------|----------|
| 10 | | | | | | | | | |
| 11 | | | | | | | | | |
| 12 | | | | | | | | | |
| 13 | | | | | | | | | |
| 14 | | | | | | | | | |
| 15 | | | | | | | | | |
| 16 | | | | | | | | | |
| 17 | | | | | | | | | |
| 18 | | | | | | | | | |
| TOTAL | | | | | | | | | |
| ROUND | | | | | | | | | |

**Summary/Practice Plan:**

DATE _____ WEATHER _____

COURSE _____ BACK TEES _____ REGULAR _____ LADIES_____

PAR_____ COURSE RATING _____ WINTER RULES _____ SUMMER RULES _____

| Hole | PAR | HDCP | Score | FH | GIR | UD | SS | Putts | Comments |
|---|---|---|---|---|---|---|---|---|---|
| 1 | | | | | | | | | |
| 2 | | | | | | | | | |
| 3 | | | | | | | | | |
| 4 | | | | | | | | | |
| 5 | | | | | | | | | |
| 6 | | | | | | | | | |
| 7 | | | | | | | | | |
| 8 | | | | | | | | | |
| 9 | | | | | | | | | |
| TOTAL | | | | | | | | | |

HDCP — Scorecard Handicap Rating     UD — Up & Down     LB— Lost Ball

FH — Fairways Hit     SS — Sand Saves     HP— Hazard Penalties

GIR — Greens In Regulation     OB — Out of Bounds     LU— Lay up

PRACTICE SITE _____

PRACTICE TYPE  (A or B) _____

NO. OF BALLS HIT_____
SHORT GAME
WEDGES ___ CHIPPING ___ PUTTING ___

PRACTICE SITE _____

PRACTICE TYPE  (A or B) _____

NO. OF BALLS HIT_____
SHORT GAME
WEDGES ___ CHIPPING ___ PUTTING ___

| Hole | PAR | HDCP | Score | FH | GIR | UD | SS | Putts | Comments |
|------|-----|------|-------|-----|-----|-----|-----|-------|----------|
| 10 | | | | | | | | | |
| 11 | | | | | | | | | |
| 12 | | | | | | | | | |
| 13 | | | | | | | | | |
| 14 | | | | | | | | | |
| 15 | | | | | | | | | |
| 16 | | | | | | | | | |
| 17 | | | | | | | | | |
| 18 | | | | | | | | | |
| TOTAL | | | | | | | | | |
| ROUND | | | | | | | | | |

**Summary/Practice Plan:**

DATE _____ WEATHER _____

COURSE _____ BACK TEES _____ REGULAR _____ LADIES_____

PAR_____ COURSE RATING _____ WINTER RULES _____ SUMMER RULES _____

| Hole | PAR | HDCP | Score | FH | GIR | UD | SS | Putts | Comments |
|------|-----|------|-------|----|----|----|----|----|----------|
| 1 | | | | | | | | | |
| 2 | | | | | | | | | |
| 3 | | | | | | | | | |
| 4 | | | | | | | | | |
| 5 | | | | | | | | | |
| 6 | | | | | | | | | |
| 7 | | | | | | | | | |
| 8 | | | | | | | | | |
| 9 | | | | | | | | | |
| TOTAL | | | | | | | | | |

HDCP — Scorecard Handicap Rating    UD — Up & Down    LB— Lost Ball
FH — Fairways Hit    SS — Sand Saves    HP— Hazard Penalties
GIR — Greens In Regulation    OB — Out of Bounds    LU— Lay up

PRACTICE SITE _____   PRACTICE SITE _____

PRACTICE TYPE  (A or B) _____   PRACTICE TYPE  (A or B) _____

NO. OF BALLS HIT_____   NO. OF BALLS HIT_____

SHORT GAME   SHORT GAME

WEDGES ___ CHIPPING ___ PUTTING ___   WEDGES ___ CHIPPING ___ PUTTING ___

| Hole | PAR | HDCP | Score | FH | GIR | UD | SS | Putts | Comments |
|------|-----|------|-------|----|----|----|----|-------|----------|
| 10 | | | | | | | | | |
| 11 | | | | | | | | | |
| 12 | | | | | | | | | |
| 13 | | | | | | | | | |
| 14 | | | | | | | | | |
| 15 | | | | | | | | | |
| 16 | | | | | | | | | |
| 17 | | | | | | | | | |
| 18 | | | | | | | | | |
| TOTAL | | | | | | | | | |
| ROUND | | | | | | | | | |

**Summary/Practice Plan:**

DATE _____ WEATHER _____

COURSE _____ BACK TEES _____ REGULAR _____ LADIES_____

PAR_____ COURSE RATING _____ WINTER RULES _____ SUMMER RULES _____

| Hole | PAR | HDCP | Score | FH | GIR | UD | SS | Putts | Comments |
|------|-----|------|-------|----|----|----|----|----|----|
| 1 | | | | | | | | | |
| 2 | | | | | | | | | |
| 3 | | | | | | | | | |
| 4 | | | | | | | | | |
| 5 | | | | | | | | | |
| 6 | | | | | | | | | |
| 7 | | | | | | | | | |
| 8 | | | | | | | | | |
| 9 | | | | | | | | | |
| TOTAL | | | | | | | | | |

HDCP — Scorecard Handicap Rating    UD — Up & Down    LB— Lost Ball
FH — Fairways Hit    SS — Sand Saves    HP— Hazard Penalties
GIR — Greens In Regulation    OB — Out of Bounds    LU— Lay up

PRACTICE SITE _____   PRACTICE SITE _____

PRACTICE TYPE  (A or B) _____   PRACTICE TYPE  (A or B) _____

NO. OF BALLS HIT_____   NO. OF BALLS HIT_____
SHORT GAME   SHORT GAME

WEDGES ___ CHIPPING ___ PUTTING ___   WEDGES ___ CHIPPING ___ PUTTING ___

| Hole | PAR | HDCP | Score | FH | GIR | UD | SS | Putts | Comments |
|---|---|---|---|---|---|---|---|---|---|
| 10 | | | | | | | | | |
| 11 | | | | | | | | | |
| 12 | | | | | | | | | |
| 13 | | | | | | | | | |
| 14 | | | | | | | | | |
| 15 | | | | | | | | | |
| 16 | | | | | | | | | |
| 17 | | | | | | | | | |
| 18 | | | | | | | | | |
| TOTAL | | | | | | | | | |
| ROUND | | | | | | | | | |

**Summary/Practice Plan:**

DATE _____ WEATHER _____

COURSE _____ BACK TEES _____ REGULAR _____ LADIES_____

PAR_____ COURSE RATING _____ WINTER RULES _____ SUMMER RULES _____

| Hole | PAR | HDCP | Score | FH | GIR | UD | SS | Putts | Comments |
|---|---|---|---|---|---|---|---|---|---|
| 1 | | | | | | | | | |
| 2 | | | | | | | | | |
| 3 | | | | | | | | | |
| 4 | | | | | | | | | |
| 5 | | | | | | | | | |
| 6 | | | | | | | | | |
| 7 | | | | | | | | | |
| 8 | | | | | | | | | |
| 9 | | | | | | | | | |
| TOTAL | | | | | | | | | |

HDCP — Scorecard Handicap Rating    UD — Up & Down    LB— Lost Ball
FH — Fairways Hit    SS — Sand Saves    HP— Hazard Penalties
GIR — Greens In Regulation    OB — Out of Bounds    LU— Lay up

PRACTICE SITE _____        PRACTICE SITE _____

PRACTICE TYPE  (A or B) _____      PRACTICE TYPE  (A or B) _____

NO. OF BALLS HIT_____      NO. OF BALLS HIT_____
SHORT GAME                            SHORT GAME

WEDGES ___ CHIPPING ___ PUTTING ___   WEDGES ___ CHIPPING ___ PUTTING ___

| Hole | PAR | HDCP | Score | FH | GIR | UD | SS | Putts | Comments |
|------|-----|------|-------|-----|-----|-----|-----|-------|----------|
| 10 | | | | | | | | | |
| 11 | | | | | | | | | |
| 12 | | | | | | | | | |
| 13 | | | | | | | | | |
| 14 | | | | | | | | | |
| 15 | | | | | | | | | |
| 16 | | | | | | | | | |
| 17 | | | | | | | | | |
| 18 | | | | | | | | | |
| TOTAL | | | | | | | | | |
| ROUND | | | | | | | | | |

**Summary/Practice Plan:**

DATE _____ WEATHER _____

COURSE _____ BACK TEES _____ REGULAR _____ LADIES_____

PAR_____ COURSE RATING _____ WINTER RULES _____ SUMMER RULES _____

| Hole | PAR | HDCP | Score | FH | GIR | UD | SS | Putts | Comments |
|------|-----|------|-------|----|----|----|----|-------|----------|
| 1 | | | | | | | | | |
| 2 | | | | | | | | | |
| 3 | | | | | | | | | |
| 4 | | | | | | | | | |
| 5 | | | | | | | | | |
| 6 | | | | | | | | | |
| 7 | | | | | | | | | |
| 8 | | | | | | | | | |
| 9 | | | | | | | | | |
| TOTAL | | | | | | | | | |

HDCP — Scorecard Handicap Rating　　UD — Up & Down　　　　LB— Lost Ball
FH — Fairways Hit　　　　　　　　　SS — Sand Saves　　　　HP— Hazard Penalties
GIR — Greens In Regulation　　　　　OB — Out of Bounds　　　LU— Lay up

PRACTICE SITE _____ | PRACTICE SITE _____

PRACTICE TYPE  (A or B) _____ | PRACTICE TYPE  (A or B) _____

NO. OF BALLS HIT_____ | NO. OF BALLS HIT_____
SHORT GAME | SHORT GAME
WEDGES ___ CHIPPING ___ PUTTING ___ | WEDGES ___ CHIPPING ___ PUTTING ___

| Hole | PAR | HDCP | Score | FH | GIR | UD | SS | Putts | Comments |
|------|-----|------|-------|----|----|----|----|----|----------|
| 10 | | | | | | | | | |
| 11 | | | | | | | | | |
| 12 | | | | | | | | | |
| 13 | | | | | | | | | |
| 14 | | | | | | | | | |
| 15 | | | | | | | | | |
| 16 | | | | | | | | | |
| 17 | | | | | | | | | |
| 18 | | | | | | | | | |
| TOTAL | | | | | | | | | |
| ROUND | | | | | | | | | |

**Summary/Practice Plan:**

DATE _____ WEATHER _____

COURSE _____ BACK TEES ____ REGULAR ____ LADIES____

PAR_____ COURSE RATING _____ WINTER RULES ____ SUMMER RULES _____

| Hole | PAR | HDCP | Score | FH | GIR | UD | SS | Putts | Comments |
|------|-----|------|-------|-----|-----|-----|-----|-------|----------|
| 1 | | | | | | | | | |
| 2 | | | | | | | | | |
| 3 | | | | | | | | | |
| 4 | | | | | | | | | |
| 5 | | | | | | | | | |
| 6 | | | | | | | | | |
| 7 | | | | | | | | | |
| 8 | | | | | | | | | |
| 9 | | | | | | | | | |
| TOTAL | | | | | | | | | |

HDCP — Scorecard Handicap Rating    UD — Up & Down    LB— Lost Ball
FH — Fairways Hit    SS — Sand Saves    HP— Hazard Penalties
GIR — Greens In Regulation    OB — Out of Bounds    LU— Lay up

PRACTICE SITE _____ | PRACTICE SITE _____

PRACTICE TYPE (A or B) _____ | PRACTICE TYPE (A or B) _____

NO. OF BALLS HIT_____ | NO. OF BALLS HIT_____

SHORT GAME | SHORT GAME

WEDGES ___ CHIPPING ___ PUTTING ___ | WEDGES ___ CHIPPING ___ PUTTING ___

| Hole | PAR | HDCP | Score | FH | GIR | UD | SS | Putts | Comments |
|------|-----|------|-------|----|----|----|----|-------|----------|
| 10 | | | | | | | | | |
| 11 | | | | | | | | | |
| 12 | | | | | | | | | |
| 13 | | | | | | | | | |
| 14 | | | | | | | | | |
| 15 | | | | | | | | | |
| 16 | | | | | | | | | |
| 17 | | | | | | | | | |
| 18 | | | | | | | | | |
| TOTAL | | | | | | | | | |
| ROUND | | | | | | | | | |

**Summary/Practice Plan:**

DATE _____ WEATHER _____

COURSE _____ BACK TEES _____ REGULAR _____ LADIES_____

PAR_____ COURSE RATING _____ WINTER RULES _____ SUMMER RULES _____

| Hole | PAR | HDCP | Score | FH | GIR | UD | SS | Putts | Comments |
|------|-----|------|-------|----|-----|----|----|-------|----------|
| 1 | | | | | | | | | |
| 2 | | | | | | | | | |
| 3 | | | | | | | | | |
| 4 | | | | | | | | | |
| 5 | | | | | | | | | |
| 6 | | | | | | | | | |
| 7 | | | | | | | | | |
| 8 | | | | | | | | | |
| 9 | | | | | | | | | |
| TOTAL | | | | | | | | | |

HDCP — Scorecard Handicap Rating    UD — Up & Down       LB— Lost Ball
FH — Fairways Hit                   SS — Sand Saves       HP— Hazard Penalties
GIR — Greens In Regulation          OB — Out of Bounds    LU— Lay up

PRACTICE SITE _____     PRACTICE SITE _____

PRACTICE TYPE  (A or B) _____     PRACTICE TYPE  (A or B) _____

NO. OF BALLS HIT_____     NO. OF BALLS HIT_____
SHORT GAME     SHORT GAME
WEDGES ___ CHIPPING ___ PUTTING ___     WEDGES ___ CHIPPING ___ PUTTING ___

| Hole | PAR | HDCP | Score | FH | GIR | UD | SS | Putts | Comments |
|------|-----|------|-------|----|----|----|----|-------|----------|
| 10 | | | | | | | | | |
| 11 | | | | | | | | | |
| 12 | | | | | | | | | |
| 13 | | | | | | | | | |
| 14 | | | | | | | | | |
| 15 | | | | | | | | | |
| 16 | | | | | | | | | |
| 17 | | | | | | | | | |
| 18 | | | | | | | | | |
| TOTAL | | | | | | | | | |
| ROUND | | | | | | | | | |

**Summary/Practice Plan:**

DATE _____ WEATHER _____

COURSE _____ BACK TEES _____ REGULAR _____ LADIES_____

PAR_____ COURSE RATING _____ WINTER RULES _____ SUMMER RULES _____

| Hole | PAR | HDCP | Score | FH | GIR | UD | SS | Putts | Comments |
|---|---|---|---|---|---|---|---|---|---|
| 1 | | | | | | | | | |
| 2 | | | | | | | | | |
| 3 | | | | | | | | | |
| 4 | | | | | | | | | |
| 5 | | | | | | | | | |
| 6 | | | | | | | | | |
| 7 | | | | | | | | | |
| 8 | | | | | | | | | |
| 9 | | | | | | | | | |
| TOTAL | | | | | | | | | |

HDCP — Scorecard Handicap Rating          UD — Up & Down          LB— Lost Ball
FH — Fairways Hit                         SS — Sand Saves         HP— Hazard Penalties
GIR — Greens In Regulation               OB — Out of Bounds      LU— Lay up

PRACTICE SITE _____ | PRACTICE SITE _____

PRACTICE TYPE (A or B) _____ | PRACTICE TYPE (A or B) _____

NO. OF BALLS HIT_____ | NO. OF BALLS HIT_____

SHORT GAME | SHORT GAME

WEDGES ___ CHIPPING ___ PUTTING ___ | WEDGES ___ CHIPPING ___ PUTTING ___

| Hole | PAR | HDCP | Score | FH | GIR | UD | SS | Putts | Comments |
|------|-----|------|-------|----|----|----|----|-------|----------|
| 10 | | | | | | | | | |
| 11 | | | | | | | | | |
| 12 | | | | | | | | | |
| 13 | | | | | | | | | |
| 14 | | | | | | | | | |
| 15 | | | | | | | | | |
| 16 | | | | | | | | | |
| 17 | | | | | | | | | |
| 18 | | | | | | | | | |
| TOTAL | | | | | | | | | |
| ROUND | | | | | | | | | |

**Summary/Practice Plan:**

DATE _____ WEATHER _____

COURSE _____ BACK TEES _____ REGULAR _____ LADIES_____

PAR_____ COURSE RATING _____ WINTER RULES _____ SUMMER RULES _____

| Hole | PAR | HDCP | Score | FH | GIR | UD | SS | Putts | Comments |
|------|-----|------|-------|-----|-----|-----|-----|-------|----------|
| 1 | | | | | | | | | |
| 2 | | | | | | | | | |
| 3 | | | | | | | | | |
| 4 | | | | | | | | | |
| 5 | | | | | | | | | |
| 6 | | | | | | | | | |
| 7 | | | | | | | | | |
| 8 | | | | | | | | | |
| 9 | | | | | | | | | |
| TOTAL | | | | | | | | | |

HDCP — Scorecard Handicap Rating UD — Up & Down LB— Lost Ball
FH — Fairways Hit SS — Sand Saves HP— Hazard Penalties
GIR — Greens In Regulation OB — Out of Bounds LU— Lay up

PRACTICE SITE _____ | PRACTICE SITE _____

PRACTICE TYPE (A or B) _____ | PRACTICE TYPE (A or B) _____

NO. OF BALLS HIT_____ | NO. OF BALLS HIT_____

SHORT GAME | SHORT GAME

WEDGES ___ CHIPPING ___ PUTTING ___ | WEDGES ___ CHIPPING ___ PUTTING ___

| Hole | PAR | HDCP | Score | FH | GIR | UD | SS | Putts | Comments |
|------|-----|------|-------|----|----|----|----|-------|----------|
| 10 | | | | | | | | | |
| 11 | | | | | | | | | |
| 12 | | | | | | | | | |
| 13 | | | | | | | | | |
| 14 | | | | | | | | | |
| 15 | | | | | | | | | |
| 16 | | | | | | | | | |
| 17 | | | | | | | | | |
| 18 | | | | | | | | | |
| TOTAL | | | | | | | | | |
| ROUND | | | | | | | | | |

**Summary/Practice Plan:**

DATE _____ WEATHER _____

COURSE _____ BACK TEES _____ REGULAR _____ LADIES_____

PAR_____ COURSE RATING _____ WINTER RULES _____ SUMMER RULES _____

| Hole | PAR | HDCP | Score | FH | GIR | UD | SS | Putts | Comments |
|-------|-----|------|-------|----|-----|----|----|-------|----------|
| 1 | | | | | | | | | |
| 2 | | | | | | | | | |
| 3 | | | | | | | | | |
| 4 | | | | | | | | | |
| 5 | | | | | | | | | |
| 6 | | | | | | | | | |
| 7 | | | | | | | | | |
| 8 | | | | | | | | | |
| 9 | | | | | | | | | |
| TOTAL | | | | | | | | | |

HDCP — Scorecard Handicap Rating        UD — Up & Down        LB— Lost Ball
FH — Fairways Hit                       SS — Sand Saves       HP— Hazard Penalties
GIR — Greens In Regulation             OB — Out of Bounds    LU— Lay up

PRACTICE SITE _____   PRACTICE SITE _____

PRACTICE TYPE  (A or B) _____   PRACTICE TYPE  (A or B) _____

NO. OF BALLS HIT_____   NO. OF BALLS HIT_____

SHORT GAME   SHORT GAME

WEDGES ___ CHIPPING ___ PUTTING ___   WEDGES ___ CHIPPING ___ PUTTING ___

| Hole | PAR | HDCP | Score | FH | GIR | UD | SS | Putts | Comments |
|------|-----|------|-------|-----|-----|-----|-----|-------|----------|
| 10 | | | | | | | | | |
| 11 | | | | | | | | | |
| 12 | | | | | | | | | |
| 13 | | | | | | | | | |
| 14 | | | | | | | | | |
| 15 | | | | | | | | | |
| 16 | | | | | | | | | |
| 17 | | | | | | | | | |
| 18 | | | | | | | | | |
| TOTAL | | | | | | | | | |
| ROUND | | | | | | | | | |

**Summary/Practice Plan:**

DATE _____ WEATHER _____

COURSE _____ BACK TEES _____ REGULAR _____ LADIES_____

PAR_____ COURSE RATING _____ WINTER RULES _____ SUMMER RULES _____

| Hole | PAR | HDCP | Score | FH | GIR | UD | SS | Putts | Comments |
|------|-----|------|-------|----|----|----|----|-------|----------|
| 1 | | | | | | | | | |
| 2 | | | | | | | | | |
| 3 | | | | | | | | | |
| 4 | | | | | | | | | |
| 5 | | | | | | | | | |
| 6 | | | | | | | | | |
| 7 | | | | | | | | | |
| 8 | | | | | | | | | |
| 9 | | | | | | | | | |
| TOTAL | | | | | | | | | |

HDCP — Scorecard Handicap Rating    UD — Up & Down    LB— Lost Ball
FH — Fairways Hit    SS — Sand Saves    HP— Hazard Penalties
GIR — Greens In Regulation    OB — Out of Bounds    LU— Lay up

PRACTICE SITE _____

PRACTICE TYPE (A or B) _____

NO. OF BALLS HIT_____
SHORT GAME
WEDGES ___ CHIPPING ___ PUTTING ___

PRACTICE SITE _____

PRACTICE TYPE (A or B) _____

NO. OF BALLS HIT_____
SHORT GAME
WEDGES ___ CHIPPING ___ PUTTING ___

| Hole | PAR | HDCP | Score | FH | GIR | UD | SS | Putts | Comments |
|------|-----|------|-------|----|----|----|----|-------|----------|
| 10 | | | | | | | | | |
| 11 | | | | | | | | | |
| 12 | | | | | | | | | |
| 13 | | | | | | | | | |
| 14 | | | | | | | | | |
| 15 | | | | | | | | | |
| 16 | | | | | | | | | |
| 17 | | | | | | | | | |
| 18 | | | | | | | | | |
| TOTAL | | | | | | | | | |
| ROUND | | | | | | | | | |

**Summary/Practice Plan:**

DATE _____ WEATHER _____

COURSE _____ BACK TEES _____ REGULAR _____ LADIES_____

PAR _____ COURSE RATING _____ WINTER RULES _____ SUMMER RULES _____

| Hole | PAR | HDCP | Score | FH | GIR | UD | SS | Putts | Comments |
|------|-----|------|-------|-----|-----|-----|-----|-------|----------|
| 1 | | | | | | | | | |
| 2 | | | | | | | | | |
| 3 | | | | | | | | | |
| 4 | | | | | | | | | |
| 5 | | | | | | | | | |
| 6 | | | | | | | | | |
| 7 | | | | | | | | | |
| 8 | | | | | | | | | |
| 9 | | | | | | | | | |
| TOTAL | | | | | | | | | |

HDCP — Scorecard Handicap Rating  UD — Up & Down  LB— Lost Ball
FH — Fairways Hit  SS — Sand Saves  HP— Hazard Penalties
GIR — Greens In Regulation  OB — Out of Bounds  LU— Lay up

PRACTICE SITE _____    PRACTICE SITE _____

PRACTICE TYPE (A or B) _____    PRACTICE TYPE (A or B) _____

NO. OF BALLS HIT_____    NO. OF BALLS HIT_____

SHORT GAME             SHORT GAME

WEDGES ___ CHIPPING ___ PUTTING ___    WEDGES ___ CHIPPING ___ PUTTING ___

| Hole | PAR | HDCP | Score | FH | GIR | UD | SS | Putts | Comments |
|------|-----|------|-------|-----|-----|-----|-----|-------|----------|
| 10 | | | | | | | | | |
| 11 | | | | | | | | | |
| 12 | | | | | | | | | |
| 13 | | | | | | | | | |
| 14 | | | | | | | | | |
| 15 | | | | | | | | | |
| 16 | | | | | | | | | |
| 17 | | | | | | | | | |
| 18 | | | | | | | | | |
| TOTAL | | | | | | | | | |
| ROUND | | | | | | | | | |

**Summary/Practice Plan:**

DATE _____ WEATHER _____

COURSE _____ BACK TEES ____ REGULAR ____ LADIES____

PAR_____ COURSE RATING _____ WINTER RULES ____ SUMMER RULES _____

| Hole | PAR | HDCP | Score | FH | GIR | UD | SS | Putts | Comments |
|------|-----|------|-------|----|----|----|----|-------|----------|
| 1 | | | | | | | | | |
| 2 | | | | | | | | | |
| 3 | | | | | | | | | |
| 4 | | | | | | | | | |
| 5 | | | | | | | | | |
| 6 | | | | | | | | | |
| 7 | | | | | | | | | |
| 8 | | | | | | | | | |
| 9 | | | | | | | | | |
| TOTAL | | | | | | | | | |

HDCP — Scorecard Handicap Rating    UD — Up & Down    LB— Lost Ball
FH — Fairways Hit    SS — Sand Saves    HP— Hazard Penalties
GIR — Greens In Regulation    OB — Out of Bounds    LU— Lay up

PRACTICE SITE _____   PRACTICE SITE _____

PRACTICE TYPE  (A or B) _____   PRACTICE TYPE  (A or B) _____

NO. OF BALLS HIT_____   NO. OF BALLS HIT_____
SHORT GAME                            SHORT GAME

WEDGES ___ CHIPPING ___ PUTTING ___   WEDGES ___ CHIPPING ___ PUTTING ___

| Hole | PAR | HDCP | Score | FH | GIR | UD | SS | Putts | Comments |
|------|-----|------|-------|----|----|----|----|-------|----------|
| 10 | | | | | | | | | |
| 11 | | | | | | | | | |
| 12 | | | | | | | | | |
| 13 | | | | | | | | | |
| 14 | | | | | | | | | |
| 15 | | | | | | | | | |
| 16 | | | | | | | | | |
| 17 | | | | | | | | | |
| 18 | | | | | | | | | |
| TOTAL | | | | | | | | | |
| ROUND | | | | | | | | | |

**Summary/Practice Plan:**

DATE _____ WEATHER _____

COURSE _____ BACK TEES _____ REGULAR _____ LADIES_____

PAR_____ COURSE RATING _____ WINTER RULES _____ SUMMER RULES _____

| Hole | PAR | HDCP | Score | FH | GIR | UD | SS | Putts | Comments |
|------|-----|------|-------|----|----|----|----|-------|----------|
| 1 | | | | | | | | | |
| 2 | | | | | | | | | |
| 3 | | | | | | | | | |
| 4 | | | | | | | | | |
| 5 | | | | | | | | | |
| 6 | | | | | | | | | |
| 7 | | | | | | | | | |
| 8 | | | | | | | | | |
| 9 | | | | | | | | | |
| TOTAL | | | | | | | | | |

HDCP — Scorecard Handicap Rating  
FH — Fairways Hit  
GIR — Greens In Regulation  

UD — Up & Down  
SS — Sand Saves  
OB — Out of Bounds  

LB— Lost Ball  
HP— Hazard Penalties  
LU— Lay up

PRACTICE SITE _____     PRACTICE SITE _____

PRACTICE TYPE (A or B) _____     PRACTICE TYPE (A or B) _____

NO. OF BALLS HIT_____     NO. OF BALLS HIT_____

SHORT GAME                        SHORT GAME

WEDGES ___ CHIPPING ___ PUTTING ___     WEDGES ___ CHIPPING ___ PUTTING ___

| Hole | PAR | HDCP | Score | FH | GIR | UD | SS | Putts | Comments |
|------|-----|------|-------|----|----|----|----|----|----------|
| 10 | | | | | | | | | |
| 11 | | | | | | | | | |
| 12 | | | | | | | | | |
| 13 | | | | | | | | | |
| 14 | | | | | | | | | |
| 15 | | | | | | | | | |
| 16 | | | | | | | | | |
| 17 | | | | | | | | | |
| 18 | | | | | | | | | |
| TOTAL | | | | | | | | | |
| ROUND | | | | | | | | | |

**Summary/Practice Plan:**

DATE _____ WEATHER _____

COURSE _____ BACK TEES _____ REGULAR _____ LADIES_____

PAR_____ COURSE RATING _____ WINTER RULES _____ SUMMER RULES _____

| Hole | PAR | HDCP | Score | FH | GIR | UD | SS | Putts | Comments |
|------|-----|------|-------|----|----|----|----|----|----------|
| 1 | | | | | | | | | |
| 2 | | | | | | | | | |
| 3 | | | | | | | | | |
| 4 | | | | | | | | | |
| 5 | | | | | | | | | |
| 6 | | | | | | | | | |
| 7 | | | | | | | | | |
| 8 | | | | | | | | | |
| 9 | | | | | | | | | |
| TOTAL | | | | | | | | | |

HDCP — Scorecard Handicap Rating     UD — Up & Down     LB— Lost Ball
FH — Fairways Hit     SS — Sand Saves     HP— Hazard Penalties
GIR — Greens In Regulation     OB — Out of Bounds     LU— Lay up

PRACTICE SITE _____   PRACTICE SITE _____

PRACTICE TYPE  (A or B) _____   PRACTICE TYPE  (A or B) _____

NO. OF BALLS HIT_____   NO. OF BALLS HIT_____

SHORT GAME   SHORT GAME

WEDGES ___ CHIPPING ___ PUTTING ___   WEDGES ___ CHIPPING ___ PUTTING ___

| Hole | PAR | HDCP | Score | FH | GIR | UD | SS | Putts | Comments |
|------|-----|------|-------|----|-----|----|----|-------|----------|
| 10 | | | | | | | | | |
| 11 | | | | | | | | | |
| 12 | | | | | | | | | |
| 13 | | | | | | | | | |
| 14 | | | | | | | | | |
| 15 | | | | | | | | | |
| 16 | | | | | | | | | |
| 17 | | | | | | | | | |
| 18 | | | | | | | | | |
| TOTAL | | | | | | | | | |
| ROUND | | | | | | | | | |

Summary/Practice Plan:

DATE _____ WEATHER _____

COURSE _____ BACK TEES _____ REGULAR _____ LADIES_____

PAR_____ COURSE RATING _____ WINTER RULES _____ SUMMER RULES _____

| Hole | PAR | HDCP | Score | FH | GIR | UD | SS | Putts | Comments |
|---|---|---|---|---|---|---|---|---|---|
| 1 | | | | | | | | | |
| 2 | | | | | | | | | |
| 3 | | | | | | | | | |
| 4 | | | | | | | | | |
| 5 | | | | | | | | | |
| 6 | | | | | | | | | |
| 7 | | | | | | | | | |
| 8 | | | | | | | | | |
| 9 | | | | | | | | | |
| TOTAL | | | | | | | | | |

HDCP — Scorecard Handicap Rating    UD — Up & Down    LB— Lost Ball
FH — Fairways Hit    SS — Sand Saves    HP— Hazard Penalties
GIR — Greens In Regulation    OB — Out of Bounds    LU— Lay up

PRACTICE SITE _____     PRACTICE SITE _____

PRACTICE TYPE (A or B) _____     PRACTICE TYPE (A or B) _____

NO. OF BALLS HIT_____     NO. OF BALLS HIT_____
SHORT GAME                               SHORT GAME
WEDGES ___ CHIPPING ___ PUTTING ___     WEDGES ___ CHIPPING ___ PUTTING ___

| Hole | PAR | HDCP | Score | FH | GIR | UD | SS | Putts | Comments |
|------|-----|------|-------|----|----|----|----|-------|----------|
| 10 | | | | | | | | | |
| 11 | | | | | | | | | |
| 12 | | | | | | | | | |
| 13 | | | | | | | | | |
| 14 | | | | | | | | | |
| 15 | | | | | | | | | |
| 16 | | | | | | | | | |
| 17 | | | | | | | | | |
| 18 | | | | | | | | | |
| TOTAL | | | | | | | | | |
| ROUND | | | | | | | | | |

**Summary/Practice Plan:**

DATE _____ WEATHER _____

COURSE _____ BACK TEES _____ REGULAR _____ LADIES _____

PAR _____ COURSE RATING _____ WINTER RULES _____ SUMMER RULES _____

| Hole | PAR | HDCP | Score | FH | GIR | UD | SS | Putts | Comments |
|------|-----|------|-------|-----|-----|-----|-----|-------|----------|
| 1 | | | | | | | | | |
| 2 | | | | | | | | | |
| 3 | | | | | | | | | |
| 4 | | | | | | | | | |
| 5 | | | | | | | | | |
| 6 | | | | | | | | | |
| 7 | | | | | | | | | |
| 8 | | | | | | | | | |
| 9 | | | | | | | | | |
| TOTAL | | | | | | | | | |

HDCP — Scorecard Handicap Rating    UD — Up & Down    LB— Lost Ball
FH — Fairways Hit    SS — Sand Saves    HP— Hazard Penalties
GIR — Greens In Regulation    OB — Out of Bounds    LU— Lay up

PRACTICE SITE _____  PRACTICE SITE _____

PRACTICE TYPE (A or B) _____  PRACTICE TYPE (A or B) _____

NO. OF BALLS HIT_____  NO. OF BALLS HIT_____

SHORT GAME                            SHORT GAME

WEDGES ___ CHIPPING ___ PUTTING ___  WEDGES ___ CHIPPING ___ PUTTING ___

| Hole | PAR | HDCP | Score | FH | GIR | UD | SS | Putts | Comments |
|------|-----|------|-------|----|----|----|----|-------|----------|
| 10 | | | | | | | | | |
| 11 | | | | | | | | | |
| 12 | | | | | | | | | |
| 13 | | | | | | | | | |
| 14 | | | | | | | | | |
| 15 | | | | | | | | | |
| 16 | | | | | | | | | |
| 17 | | | | | | | | | |
| 18 | | | | | | | | | |
| TOTAL | | | | | | | | | |
| ROUND | | | | | | | | | |

**Summary/Practice Plan:**

# Chapter 5

## SHORT-GAME PRACTICE . . .
## DISTANCE AND IMAGINATION . . .
## BEST PUTTERS DON'T CARE . . .
## THE FUNDAMENTALS . . .

Some of my fondest memories in golf are of those long summer evenings of boyhood, just me, my clubs and six balls and the golf course, trying things. I put those balls in weird places, just to see if I could hit the shot, see if I could do it. Actually, I developed a decent short game in those delicious days.

My first year on Tour I won two tournaments. I really feel that practicing the short game the way I did growing up gave me an advantage. Not many worked on the short game back then. But once I hit the Tour, different deal. They kind of frown on playing six balls on every hole in a practice round, trying weird shots when the mood hits you. There weren't many practice facilities around then where you could work on your short game. Not true today.

So my short game began to suffer.

Then one day I watched Jim Simons practice on the range, doing something I had never seen before. He would send his caddie out to the corner of the range. His caddie would toss down a few towels as targets, then stand off to the side and yell numbers back at Simons — usually something like 40, 60 and 80.

Simons would hit one to the 40-yard target, and the caddie would yell back, "Thirty-eight." The next shot, the caddie might say, "Forty-three." Simons wanted to know the exact distance he was hitting this wedge. How far did it fly? Was it two yards short? Three yards long? Did it land right at 40 yards?

He wanted to know immediately how far the ball went so he could learn to judge the speed and length he needed to swing the club to produce a 40-yard shot. Then he would do the same thing with the 60-yard shot and the 80-yard shot. This was a new way

Learn the "feel" it takes to hit a sand or pitching wedge exactly 50 yards. I see this as critical to better scoring. By "exactly" I do mean *exactly*.

to practice the short stuff. Made sense to me.

Simons no longer plays the Tour. But he was a darn good player. Nearly won the U.S. Open as an amateur in college. He was a guy who had the work ethic of a Tom Kite, but not quite Tom's talent.

The biggest mistakes in wedge play are always in distance control. If you really want to improve your overall game, and lower your scores, the short game is the shortcut. Find out for yourself how important wedge play is by using the charts I put in this book. Just count up how many times you use a club from the wedge family in a round of golf. You might be amazed. Around the greens, the wedge is apt to be your worst nightmare before it becomes your best friend.

Ben Hogan called his wedge the "Equalizer." And that's what it is, one of the most powerful weapons in the bag. A good wedge player can equalize any shortcomings in his long game with his short game. And the key to wedge practice is distance.

Distance, distance, distance. I cannot stress it enough. Know what a 40-yard shot is. Know a 20-yard shot. A 60-yard shot. Get that down. This is practice any golfer can do. Not every golfer can hit the ball as far as Tiger Woods can or as relentlessly straight as Ben Hogan did. But any golfer can hit the ball 40 yards. Learn how to use that wedge.

Not many taught the short game

when I turned pro. Paul Runyan was always considered the best. Nobody taught putting. That was a mystery.

Chi Chi Rodriguez always said that he never practiced putting because it was all feel. One day it's there, the next . . . who knows? That kind of summed up the feeling on Tour. Either you had it or you didn't, and that was that. We just kind of accepted putting that way, more than practicing it.

That's not to say we didn't look for answers to the putting mysteries. It's just that those answers were hard to find. We were on our own. We just seemed to keep coming up with some rather desperate solutions.

In 1999, a rookie named Notah Begay came to the Tour. He putts both left-handed and right-handed, depending on the way the putt breaks. I've got news for young Mr. Begay: He is not the first — I just happen to have that dubious distinction. At least it made for good television.

The way I figured out putting was by taking a look at the best putters out there, trying to figure out what they were doing. But you couldn't ask. Putting involved secrets, sacred territory. You didn't go there. Major league guesswork is what it was.

Putting was a puzzle. You would have to go to mysterious people to learn, if you dared. Guys like George Lowe, an old hustler who lived down in Florida and was one of the best putters who ever lived. Supposedly he taught Nicklaus how to putt.

The story goes that you gave Lowe a hundred bucks for a lesson. Then he would ask you to reach into your pocket for a coin. You did. He would point out that the coin was between your thumb and index finger. He would say you brought the coin out with your thumb and index finger because that is where your feel is. And that is how you putt.

A true Range Rat is at home on the putting green, too.

99

With the thumb and index finger. End of lesson.

All feel, any way you look at it. No fundamentals that I heard.

When feel, methods and secrets overwhelm fundamentals, there's not much to practice. Solid practice means practicing fundamentals, I believe. The cold fact of the matter is that most of us simply did not know how to practice putting because we had no real fundamentals.

Oh, we knew a few. The Vardon reverse overlap grip was a standard. That put all the fingers of the right hand on the putter for better feel, while keeping the back of the left hand solid so the stroke wouldn't break down. But you would also see split-hand grips, cross-handed grips and sidesaddle grips. They all worked, for the most part. For a while.

Take a fundamental like the stance. There are as many putting stances on Tour as there are putters, same as it was when I came up. We just went with what we thought worked. If we saw an amateur partner in the Wednesday pro-am sink some serious footage, in the evening we would try that stance.

Lots of guesswork. Not good.

Don January, a great putter, stands upright. Hubie Green, a superb putter, hunches over the ball with his feet wide apart. Lee Trevino has an open stance, with the ball so far back it is almost off his right foot. Bobby Locke had a closed stance. Sam Snead, the gifted man with the best swing in golf, adopted the ugli-est putting stance ever. Awful. He invented sidesaddle after croquet-style was outlawed by the USGA.

So where were the fundamentals? Certainly not in the stance. And many of us would change our putting stances more often than we changed skivvies.

The putting myth died a hard death, just as the myth that the golf swing was all feel and method died a hard death. Hogan shattered all the old golf-swing axioms, but Hogan had the most serious case of the putting yips ever recorded. What that did was enhance the putting mysteries.

It stayed that way until a guy named Dave Pelz came around. He was the first to come forward with solid putting fundamentals that stuck. Once a pretty good amateur player in the Washington, D.C. area, Pelz is the first to say that he is a most unlikely guy to be dispensing putting wisdom to Tour pros.

But he is the fellow who taught Kite before Kite won the 1992 U.S. Open. He also tutored Peter Jacobsen. When Jake won a couple of tournaments in 1995, that really turned our heads. Kite is one thing. But good old Jake had been a cadaver in spikes.

Pelz specializes in the short game. Specialists meet skeptics on Tour. If we've got something that works, we're not about to change it, at least not right away. Then again, we're talking about a bunch of geniuses who took a decade or more to catch on to the way Nicklaus practiced the golf swing. Fact is, most of us did not have a putting stroke or stance that lasted long anyway. So we

## TIPS ON CHARTING . . .

- MARK DOWN IF THE SHOT WAS LEFT, RIGHT, SHORT OR LONG.
- IDENTIFY A MISSED GREEN — WAS IT ON THE FRINGE OR IN THE ROUGH?
- IDENTIFY A MISSED FAIRWAY — WAS IT ON THE FIRST CUT OR IN THE TREES?
- BUNKER SHOT — HOW DID IT GET THERE?
- MARK DOWN HOW MANY TIMES YOU USED YOUR SAND WEDGE.
- MARK DOWN HOW MANY STROKES INVOLVED THE SHORT GAME.
- IDENTIFY THREE-PUTTS — HOW MANY WERE 90-FOOTERS, HOW MANY 30-FOOTERS?
- IF YOU HIT A SIGNIFICANT NUMBER OF GREENS, YOU WILL HAVE MORE PUTTS.
- IF YOU MISS GREENS, YOU SHOULD HAVE FEWER PUTTS.

muttered a lot. We "sputtered," you could say.

Pelz sparked a revolution. We all began spending more time around the putting green. Chipping greens suddenly began popping up in practice areas. We used them. The Pelz fundamentals became a standard. Finally.

Practice, too, is all about knowing fundamentals (I intend to keep saying it until you get tired of reading it). First and foremost, make sure you are fundamentally sound when you practice putting. Go to a pro who knows how to teach putting. Or read the Pelz book. Once you learn the fundamentals, practice those fundamentals. Practice them hard if you intend to improve your game substantially.

I have talked about two different kinds of practice. One is used to carry your game from the practice tee to the golf course. The other type of practice involves swing mechanics. Both of these practice sessions are applicable as well to putting. But remember, it is one or the other. The two practice sessions do not mix. Capiche?

If you come back from seeing your teaching pro with a new putting stance, you'll have to practice that stance for awhile before it feels like a habit. You may come back with a taller stance so that your arms can hang down, and you may feel like you are a mile from the ball. Pay no attention to where the ball goes. Learning a new position is your goal, remember, not making the putt. Pay no attention to whether the ball goes into the cup for . . . how long did I say? That's right, at least 21 days. This is of paramount importance in putting practice.

With all the technical stuff a teacher

101

like Pelz can throw at you, from the physics of how a blade of grass will react to a balata ball to moments of inertia in a pendulum swing, he came up with one beautiful precept — "golfers who don't care never get the yips."

Don't ask me how he came up with that one from his data, but he did. And it fits. It makes sense.

I've always thought that golf is a weird game that way. When you hit a shot you have got to care, but once the ball is in the air you can't care. Once the ball has left the clubface it is out of your control. To play this game in a way that you have your emotions in check, you have to accept wherever the ball ends up. In modern lingo, deal with it. Live with it. Get over it.

To me, that's the same thing as the Pelz precept. Saying that those who don't care never get the yips, to me, is the same thing as saying you can't care where the ball goes once you've hit it.

And this is something you can practice. Use the practice session involving swing mechanics. Part of that practice session is not caring where the ball goes. That's the kicker — you also are practicing the mind-set of not caring once the ball is gone. Get to that point and it is sayonara yips.

Just as with the wedge, distance is key in putting. Work on speed. Don't care

Practice putting, yes, but be sure your technique is solid. They're working hard at Buchanan Fields Municipal in Concord, California.

**Chipping and pitching are parts of the game that bedevil many amateurs. The answer? Practice, of course.**

whether the ball goes into the cup, because that's not the goal. The goal is to get the ball about a foot on the other side of the cup. That's the proper speed.

When I apply the practice session that involves target and ball flight to putting, I think about pitching pennies. Do you look at your hand when you're pitching a penny? How tight do you hold the penny? How firm is your arm? How big is your arm swing? Well, who the hell knows?

I don't think anybody thinks about those things when they pitch pennies. Do you? I think they look at the target, imagine what kind of force it will take to pitch the penny to the target, and no more. How tight you hold it, how free or how long are your arm swings, all that will take care of itself. Same thing in putting.

Think like a basketball player. When he goes up for a shot he's not worried about where his left elbow is or how high off the ground he's going to jump. He is thinking about the hoop. That's it. And that's Practice A.

Remember that a golf swing can repair itself as if by magic with good timing and rhythm. Like the cat that always lands on its feet, there's something inside us that will make the necessary adjustments to make that ball go towards the hole without having to think about it.

This type of practice, Practice A, also gets a golfer away from the most dangerous thing he or she can do in practice, which is internalizing and rationalizing right up to a Hogan putting freeze. Paralysis by analysis is a rampant virus on the putting green.

103

Think about the cup, orient yourself there with a good stance, and the body will make the necessary adjustments to send the ball where it is supposed to go. Trust it.

Learn the fundamentals and practice them, then on Game Day think target and trust your instincts.

With all due respect to Dave Pelz, this is not nuclear science we are dealing with here. Especially with putting, a golfer can be overloaded with technical gobbledygook. Sometimes we golfers think too much. We try to be too exact, and before you know it we can't play the game.

Imagine if a guy playing pool at a local tavern went through what we do in putting. It has never happened, has it? Ever see a guy playing nine-ball get the yips? Now that would be a sorry sight. And cause for yet another firestorm of self-help books.

I have never seen a pocket billiards player lose his stroke. He's not thinking about his stroke. He's thinking about what's in front of him, as athletes do in other sports. His concern is moving the cue ball to a certain point with a certain amount of speed, not how he's holding the darn cue stick. Billy Casper, one of the best putters I've ever seen, has a pool table at home. He uses the pool table so the same idea carries over to his putting.

A lot of learning how to practice is learning how to use the mind. Think target and the mind clicks on instinct. Think swing mechanics, and the mind will say, "Be careful, you incompetent slug. Don't do anything stupid." That is why it is important to create a habit first, so you don't have to think about swing mechanics while you are playing golf.

Please tell me I am beginning to get through to you about Practice A and Practice B.

The scientific approach to this game

## TRUST YOUR OWN STYLE

IF YOU LIKE THE GAME AND HAVE PLAYED IT A WHILE, AND EVEN IF YOU HAVE ONLY A MODICUM OF ATHLETIC TALENT, BY NOW YOU HAVE DEVELOPED YOUR OWN STYLE. I CALL IT A "THUMB PRINT." NO MATTER WHAT YOU HEAR OR READ ELSEWHERE, YOU SIMPLY ARE NOT GOING TO SUBSTANTIALLY ALTER THAT THUMB PRINT. IT IS HOW YOU LEARNED TO HIT THE BALL AND IT IS AS INGRAINED AS DINNER TIME. ADJUSTMENTS, NEW SWING POSITIONS, YES, BUT EVEN THOSE TAKE 21 DAYS OF WORK, AS I HAVE SAID. BUT STAY WITH YOUR BASIC SWING, YOUR THUMB PRINT. FOR EVERY PERSON WHO TRIES TO SCRAP EVERYTHING AND DEVELOP A TOTALLY NEW SWING, I WILL SHOW YOU A DOZEN CANDIDATES FOR THE NC (NO CARD) WARD AT THE GOLF HOSPITAL.

has always appealed to me because I believe in proven fundamentals and cold, hard numbers. Dave Pelz gave us proven fundamentals for putting. Use them in practice. But also practice the game.

When Tiger Woods made his pro debut in Milwaukee, one day the TV camera caught Tiger and Brad Faxon having friendly competition with their sand wedges around the practice green. Like a couple of kids after school, they were playing You Can't Top This. They were coming up with the most imaginative shots they could think of to try to top each another. Some day that little session may pay off for one of them.

Woods likes to use a 3-wood to chip or putt from the long grass by the green. This is one very effective shot. How do you think he came up with that one? Well, one day as he was practicing flop wedge shots from long grass, the light bulb in the cranium came on. Just for the heck of it, he thought it might be fun to try a 3-wood from that position. And it worked.

Creativity in practice. And now he's got a new, effective shot in his arsenal. The whole thing reminds me one more time of those boyhood evenings when I would go to the golf course and try shots from impossible lies.

How does this kind of practice work? Experiment. Have fun. Learn. See what you can come up with. Practice isn't always about creating a habit. It is also about coming up with something new to add to your arsenal. The shots I see

## 10 BEST SHORT GAMES ON TOUR . . .

- TOM KITE
- TIGER WOODS
- PHIL MICKELSON
- DAVID DUVAL
- PAYNE STEWART
- PAUL AZINGER
- LOREN ROBERTS
- BERNHARD LANGER
- LARRY MIZE
- DAVIS LOVE III

amateurs most often screw up — by far — are the ones around the greens. Why? Because they never practice them. No clue as to what to do when they get into trouble. Then it's Triple Bogey City.

Some of this stuff can best be learned under the eyes of your teacher. If you don't know the fundamentals and the various techniques with sand play, for example, then the only logical answer is to stay out of the bunkers. Not very realistic, you say?

Most amateurs have a pet club they use for chipping, usually one of their wedges. I have seen some really good chippers do that. But the best chippers use different clubs for different situations, and they have learned what to do and what to hit by experimenting. The best chippers know the rule — get that ball on the ground as soon as you can.

Once the ball starts rolling, decent results are in your favor.

Let's say I've got 40 feet of green and I'm trying to use a sand iron from eight feet off the green. If I miss-hit or mis-judge that sand iron, then my downside, my miss, might be 20 feet from the hole. But if I am using a 7-iron any misses become so much better. So, I am controlling the downside.

Always try to land the ball on a level place just on the front of the green. Create that situation in practice and see how far each ball rolls with each club. Experiment. Give yourself a feel for it by carrying the ball 10 feet with the 7-iron, landing it on the green, and then see how far it rolls, maybe 35 to 40 feet. Try an 8-iron and see how far that rolls. Try a 6-iron.

The rule of thumb is a 9-iron pitch from off the green will basically run as far as it traveled in the air. But I would learn that for myself; don't merely take my word for it. A golfer needs to learn how these things work. And imagination and experimentation around the greens is a large part of learning it all. Dave Pelz and others have now given the game bonafide fundamentals for the short game.

Might be a good idea to learn them all.

# Chapter 6

## TARGET-SPECIFIC WITH YOUR IRONS . . . KNOW DISTANCES TO GET THE BALL HOLE-HIGH . . . RANGE RATS LOVE DRILLS . . .

I went to see my instructor, Peter Kostis, early one morning at Boca Sound in Florida. There was only one other soul out that early, a guy 75 yards or so from me at the end of the range.

Peter came out in a cart and asked if I had met Franz. I said, "Franz who?" He pointed to the guy on the range. "That's Franz Klammer, the great Austrian downhill skier," he said. Really? So I got to meet the Olympic champion.

Franz may have been an Olympic downhill skiing champ, but he had a terrible habit of coming way out over the top of the swing and cutting across the ball. Peter had a solution. He had brought with him a piece of lumber, about four feet long. He turned the two-by-four up on its side and set it down close to the ball, opposite Franz.

Then he told Franz to try hitting balls without hitting the two-by-four.

Now Franz would have to keep the path of the clubhead straight. If he went outside the line at all, he would hit the two-by-four.

But Franz froze. Same guy who likes to go 400 miles an hour on slats down an icy mountain. He stared hard at that piece of lumber. "This looks pretty dangerous," he said somberly.

I almost lost it. Peter also was trying to suppress a big laugh. The two-by-four is part of a technique drill. When Peter explained this to Klammer, there were no problems. Klammer was quite familiar with technique drills from his competitive skiing days. Peter got Franz to "change his perception."

Before Kostis became my instructor, I read his comments with sports psychologist Bob Rotella in a *Golf Digest* column dealing with the development of sport-specific drills for golf. It all made sense. Golf was the only sport that had

## 13 WAYS TO IDENTIFY A REAL RANGE RAT . . .

1. TALKS ON THE RANGE.
2. HELPS OTHERS WITH THEIR SWINGS.
3. WILLING TO ACCEPT HELP.
4. KNOWS WHAT HAPPENED ON THE COURSE THAT DAY.
5. PRACTICES FOR 40 MINUTES, THEN SITS WITH OTHERS.
6. KNOWS THE CURRENT BRANDS OF GRAPHITE SHAFTS.
7. LOTS OF TAGS AND TOWELS ON BAG.
8. SECRETLY BELIEVES HE COULD WIN THE U.S. AMATEUR WITH A BREAK OR TWO.
9. KNOWS HOW TO BUILD A SWING STATION.
10. CAN TALK FUNDAMENTALS ALL DAY.
11. KNOWS THE RULES OF GOLF COLD.
12. TENACITY — ABSOLUTELY NEVER GIVES UP.
13. JUST AS HAPPY ON THE RANGE AS THE GOLF COURSE.

no outstanding technique drills, apart from a van load of gimmicks. The Range Rat has been kind of stuck just beating balls. There are other ways to practice that make sense.

I remember watching Lee Trevino take a range ball and step on it with his right foot. He would then stand on it with the outside of his foot, and that way nearly all his weight was on the inside of his right foot.

The first time I asked him about it, he chattered away as usual. "You think this is some sort of trick shot?" Lee said with mock indignation. "Man, you just don't know this game at all, do you? Watch this."

Then he took out his driver and ripped a few perfect fades.

"I shouldn't tell you what this is all about," the Merry Mex told me. "You're kind of young. But now you know how I keep the weight on the inside of my right foot on the backswing. Now, don't you go tell anybody."

Right. Me?

Just a couple of decades ago technique drills were so foreign to golf they were considered either brilliant secrets or utter madness. But that ball under Lee's right foot was, for him, an exercise in changing his own perception so he could get used to the weight on the inside of his back foot during the backswing. An excellent drill. And a lesson for a young player.

Right. Me.

The long game has a lot more to it

these days than just beating balls on the range. When I practice hitting irons, I work hard on my style because now the target becomes specific. When you look down a fairway from the tee with a driver in your hands, you're looking at a landing area about 30 or 35 yards wide. But what's a cup? About four and a quarter inches. That is what you are aiming at with an iron. Not a fairway, but the flagstick and the cup. Whole different deal.

There needs to be an understanding of how important it is to get the ball hole-high on the green with approach shots. When you practice the iron game, practice getting the ball hole-high. Hit right to your target, not short or long. Don't just fire aimlessly away. That does you no good at all.

Remember that nobody ever got paid for how *far* he or she could hit a 7-iron. What counts is how close to the target you can get your golf ball. Whether it's a "5" on the bottom of the club or an "8" on the bottom of the club, the iron game is not a strength contest. It is accuracy and finesse. You must think that way always when you pull out any iron. Always!

On the range, find out how far you hit your 7-iron. Work on your *real* distances with your irons, not your macho distances.

If you use the charts I put in this book and chart out your rounds, you

"Have a plan when you practice," as I am telling Olympic's John Flanagan. "Don't just machine-gun balls out there."

might notice that some of your irons are not going the distance you expect. Put a little note in the comment box. Scribble down whether that approach shot was short or long. Then, having charted several rounds, count up how many times you were short of the pin, how many times you were long. Now you know something specific about how far you hit a certain iron, and therefore you know what to practice. And what club to hit for whatever distance. Trust the facts.

It is far better to be over the green than short of it. Most trouble is in front of greens, not behind. That is how architects make the game visually intimidating — by putting a lot of trouble in front of a green so you can see it.

Golf is like a 7,000-yard chess game. It is moving your piece from point A to point B. With that in mind, when you practice, the idea is to have specific shots in mind, specific targets in mind. Never just snatch an iron from your bag and aim blankly at the huge field in front of you. That does exactly zip for your game. You are merely grooving mistakes. Perfect practice, remember?

Have a specific spot where you want the ball to come down. If the driving range you use doesn't have flag sticks or signs at which to aim, find one that does. Or find a spot on the range to hit to, but identify it somehow as a target. All of this is absolutely critical if you seriously intend to lower your handicap or play at some higher, more enjoyable level.

## A GOOD RANGE HAS . . .

- REAL GRASS.
- GOOD, CLEAN GOLF BALLS.
- TARGETS.
- COMFORTABLE BENCHES.
- "LASERED" DISTANCES IN EVERY STALL.
- GOOD SIGHT LINES.
- SHORT-GAME PRACTICE AREA.
- A WELL-KEPT "FAST" PUTTING GREEN.
- FREE SODAS.
- DECENT FRENCH FRIES.
- A PGA TEACHING PRO.
- CURRENT GOLF MAGAZINES.
- VIDEO/COMPUTER SWING ANALYSIS.
- A SPECIAL AREA FOR JUNIOR GOLFERS.
- A CLUB-REPAIR FACILITY.

When I practice my irons, I imagine holes on the golf course. I try shots that are required to play those holes. I'm trying to let my imagination make it all happen, picturing the shot in the air and how it should look, letting it transfer itself to my swing.

Practice this on the golf course as well as on the range. Learn your distances, just as you did with the wedge game. There is much practice that is good to do on the practice tee, and there is so much that needs to be done out on the golf course.

110

If you get a chance to go out to play by yourself now and then — late afternoons or early mornings — drop a few balls and hit different clubs from the same distance and see where they go. Be satisfied with whatever those numbers are. That's how you do it. I wish I could provide a shortcut for you, but there is none. You just have to learn what you can do, how far you hit each club, especially the wedges. You have to know your game. Otherwise, be happy with your Saturday 93 and go home.

Johnny Miller was the best iron player I ever saw.

Miller practiced like anybody else, but he was no Range Rat. He was more one of those expressive types, like Seve Ballesteros, who got bored easily on the range. Some pros could be quite satisfied staying on the range all day. They are in Range Rat Heaven. But not Miller. He got his jollies out on the course, and a lot of his practice was done on the course, hitting several shots on every hole.

Johnny hit the ball straighter than anybody I ever saw. When he was really going well, in the mid-1970s, he and his caddie, Andy Martinez, would argue over half yards. Half yards! Now, did the rest of the Tour think that was a bunch of bull? You bet. "I'm gonna hit this one a half-yard to the left, like Miller," some comedian on the range would crack to everyone's amusement. But I won't ever argue with the fact that Johnny hit it closer to the hole than anybody. He knew his distances.

When you practice your irons, hit the ball to your specific distance. You want to get the ball hole-high with the irons. *Hole-high!* For those who have never heard the story, a very young Ben Crenshaw is playing a social round with Ben Hogan. Hole after hole, as the story goes, Crenshaw is short or barely on the green facing long chips or long putts every time, and Hogan always is hole-high or slightly past it.

"Hit the ball up to the hole, young man," says Hogan. "You meet a better class of people up here." Okay, that pretty much covers it. I certainly can't say it any better.

Technique drills with the irons help prepare your game. They also help you look good as a Range Rat. Confound your fellow Rats with some of these drills. Act like Trevino, as if it all were some great secret. Range Rats love something new. They will be on you like hair on a gorilla, as Trevino would say.

Building a station, as I talked about in Chapter 3, is one drill that will make you look like a Tour pro. It is a drill to help with your alignment. Put the two clubs down on the ground, one in front of your toes, the grip end pointing to the target. The other club is perpendicular — from the golf ball to your left heel (the opposite for left-handers, of course). Now, take your stance and you are aligned, assuming your shoulders, hips and knees also are on a line parallel to the club at your toes. Now all you have to work on is distance.

## A Range Rat has
## in the car . . .

- A copy of Ben Hogan's *Five Lessons.*
- At least three backup drivers.
- A swing-position device that looks like he's into bondage.
- A shag bag.
- A new or old graphite shaft.
- At least four putters.
- At least five wedges.
- A video camera.
- Current *Golf World* and *Golf Week* magazines.
- A binocular-like distance gauge.
- An old parking pass to a PGA Tour event.
- A gift visor from a charity scrambles tournament won by a team 34 under par.

The major problem with alignment in golf is that we stand off to the side of the target line. The target line runs straight through the golf ball directly to the target. So we're standing off to the side of it. That means we're getting an oblique look at the target line. For some that can really mess with your head. And with your swing. Ah, but I have a drill for that, too.

What you do is find a club you broke somewhere along the way, take that shaft and stick it into the ground at an angle away from the ball, and in front of the ball, on your target line. The shaft should look as if it is a launch ramp in front of the ball.

Now you have a sight line, angling up to the target with an angle close to the flight of the ball as you launch it. That intermediate aiming device gives you a great idea of the line as you look up to your target. That's where I want the ball to start on its flight. That is the path on which I want the club as you swing. It is a great reinforcement to alignment.

There is a drill I use that usually gets considerable attention on the range — the astoundingly famous Roger Maltbie Claw Drill. When the lads on Tour ask about it, though, I usually tell them it is just a new grip I am trying out. Drives 'em crazy.

I have always had a tough time with grip pressure with my right hand. I have a tendency to grab the grip and squeeze. So, Peter Kostis gave me this drill. I put my left hand on the club, as usual. With the right hand, I take the first and middle fingers and place them over the shaft so the shaft runs right between those two fingers. Sort of a claw effect. Now I can't exert any pressure on to the club with my right hand. So it takes the tension out. You get a new "feel," therefore.

There are a multitude of gadget drills — with expensive equipment — you may wish to look into as well. You are on your own with this stuff. Whatever works, I say. All of these technique drills have their limits. Take them for what they are. Understand that they're just drills.

I never hit a lot of shots with my driver on the range because they tire me out. I think practicing the driver changes my rhythm and tempo. If you hit enough drivers, I promise that you will begin to swing harder and harder with each ball. After two dozens balls, you are swinging right out of your shoes.

But there is a way to use the driver much more effectively in practice. If you want to work on tempo — and you should — hit a driver and then hit a wedge. Then hit a driver, then a wedge. Back and forth, never changing that order and trying to marry the timing and the effort level of the two swings. A happy medium, let's say.

Practicing only a driver is a different deal, and you must remember that. It is a different motion. The club is longer, the swing more round. The tee shot with the driver is the only time the ball sits up on a tee, free of any grassy obstructions. So inviting is the ball on a tee that you have this tremendous urge, sometimes, just to whale on it. Not so when you have to capture the ball off turf. With the driver, and with your ball teed up, the idea is not to strike the ground at any time. If you do, bid adieu to any chance of success. Or for sure you won't get away with it often.

As you work down through your personal cadences for each club in your bag, the shafts get longer and have less loft. And the swing gets bigger and

harder. On the practice tee with a driver, it sometimes gets to be so much fun just to grip it and rip it. Unwittingly you get faster and faster. Bad idea.

After I have hit a few drivers, I've got to slow down my swing before I leave the range. As I have said, I grab my wedge, get back that lazy feeling, get that tempo back before I leave for the first tee. When you are practicing with

His friends at the Olympic Club say "Flan" is the "Range Rat King" who speaks of putting as "The Dark Side." So he hits golf balls for hours. Uh, well, okay.

your driver, or warming up before your name is called on the first tee, break up the driver sequence with intermittent 7-iron or 8-iron shots.

There is a drill I like a lot to reinforce the need for turning your body on the backswing, instead of swaying or sliding away from the ball. Hit golf balls with your feet together. It is a wonderful drill that also helps your timing. You will notice that you cannot hit it as hard or swing as fast, but that is the whole point — to slow you down and make you swing within your limits. This drill also makes it impossible to slide.

Sliding backward or forward is a common error among amateurs. It is hard to play well with that golf affliction — sliding or swaying.

By far the greatest aid to enhance techniques (Practice B, remember?) is videotape. Biomechanics and anatomical positions exposed on tape have replaced "secrets" and methods. The drills I have outlined support the technology, the advanced tape machines that erase any doubt as to what you are doing right or wrong in your swing. These machines are the lie detectors of golf.

"RANGE RATS"

# Chapter 7

# THE PRE-SHOT ROUTINE . . .
# IT'S ALL ABOUT REPETITION . . .
# PULLING THE TRIGGER . . .
# FLANAGAN SAW 'THE DARK SIDE' . . .

The two biggest breakthroughs I've had in learning how to practice this game both happened at Augusta National. Maybe there's something in the air there at Augusta. Maybe these ideas came bounding out of my subconscious in the night, thanks to some runaway adrenaline. Tough for me to explain. Nice place for it to happen, though.

My biggest breakthrough, remember, was at the 1987 Masters. That was the year I came into the Masters looking for a swing road map. I had flat lost it.

I found it by learning a new way to practice this game, a practice so effective it took me from a guy who was looking at hitting the road early to a guy who actually hit the leader board on the weekend. The last thing on my mind when I drove up Magnolia Lane that year was reaching the top of the leader board on Sunday. But I actually knocked in a putt on the ninth green to take the lead on Sunday. I finished one stroke out of the playoff. I am still fascinated.

What I had done before that Masters was mix up the two different types of practice, and it made me a mess. My swing was internalized chaos because I was trying to get my game from the practice tee to the golf course by working on swing mechanics. That just does not work, I don't care who you are.

I found out that if I just concentrated on target and ball flight in practice I could get back to playing the game again and away from my own head. I found out if I just thought about good rhythm, tempo and balance, my swing could magically repair itself. Instinct could take over. And, trust me, it did.

But that was not my first lesson on

how to get the game from the practice tee to the golf course. I had played in my first Masters 11 years earlier, and I learned an equally important lesson about practice then. I was paired with Billy Casper in the 1976 Masters, and I saw him do something I had never seen before.

Something had disturbed Casper as he was preparing to make a shot from the fairway. Billy abruptly stopped, paused a couple of seconds, then put the club back into the bag. Next, he pulled the yardage book from his hip pocket, glanced at it, went back to the bag, pulled out the same club, then hit the shot.

Now, that was interesting, I thought. I asked him about it after the round. He said, "That was my pre-shot routine."

Pre-shot routine? Well, how about that! Never really heard of that one before. I had heard about a waggle, but not a swing routine that began with pulling the yardage book out of your back pocket.

Casper's swing actually started, mentally, when he pulled the club out of the bag. Everything he did from that point on was all part of his swing, just as much as the backswing or the follow-through. So when his procedure was interrupted, he had to start over again.

After Casper told me that, I went to watch two legendary veterans, Julius Boros and Sam Snead. I watched those guys, and I swear you could set a stopwatch from the time each planted his right foot and the time he drew his club

back. And it looked so easy. Flash! It was over in a second. Every time.

They each had a pre-shot routine. They actually started the mental and physical process of swinging the club before they took their stances. Same thing every time. Right foot down, set the feet, waggle the club, right into the backswing. Same, identical movements every time. Always right on the beat. Step in, set, look, waggle waggle, go. Step in, set, look, waggle waggle, go.

That certainly made it look easier to pull the trigger. The swing started when Casper, a great player in his day, pulled a club out of the bag. I was rapt, totally hooked. Paying strict attention, I also noticed that those guys nearly always had that club moving. Or if the club wasn't moving, something was moving — like the feet. These guys were always moving at the ball. They never just stood there. Same way every time. Repetition. You had to look for it to know they were doing it

It all made sense to me. Muscles that stop are rigid muscles. As long as muscles move, there can't be that much tension. So I developed for myself a pre-shot routine. Actually, I probably already had the beginnings of one, and I didn't even know it. Most good players do. But, remember, this was only my second year on Tour. I wanted a pre-shot routine I could rely on, one that for me created a habit and gave me a sense that I knew what the hell I was doing out there.

I worked on establishing a routine

that started with putting my right foot up to the ball and the club behind the ball. Move the feet, couple of waggles, then right into the backswing.

The key to the whole deal was to do the same thing every time. Approach the ball the same way every time, have the same number of waggles every time, move the feet the same way every time. I practiced, tried moving my feet three times, waggling twice; waggling once, moving my feet twice . . . until I found a set of moves that felt comfortable. Then, on the range, I practiced until I was a zombie trying to turn a pre-shot routine into a mere habit.

I would wager a milkshake or two this is the first time someone has ever told you to practice the delicate, highly personal process of getting ready to hit the ball.

I must emphasize that this is one of those practice sessions where, in the early stages, you can't give a flip where the ball goes. The whole idea, first, is to turn those comfortable moves into a habit, not worry yet about ball flight.

It took awhile before it all came together for me. But once it became habit, it was found money. It was like one-two-three-boom! The ball's gone. All a process. No thinking and getting paralyzed over the ball. Those days were gone. Hallelujah! I felt like the character Jack Dawson in the movie *Titanic* — "I'm the king of the world!"

The pre-shot routine takes a while to learn, sort of like mastering the grip. But once it becomes habit, that's that. I

Jim Lucius is the head professional at the Olympic Club. His pre-shot routine: First he "steps in" to get ball position . . .

haven't had a conscious thought about how I put my hands on the club in 30 years. That's how the pre-shout routine works. It is critical, and it must be practiced, ingrained. I am speaking of golfers at any level. No pre-shot routine down pat, and your quest to improve will be about 10 times more difficult. Bet the ranch on it.

We hear about the pre-shot routine

all the time from my announcer pals on TV, but in a sense it may be the best kept secret in the game. At least the amateur men and women I see — particularly young players — pay little or no attention to it.

If you will discipline yourself to do something the same way over and over it will become habit after about 21 days. Trust ol' Roger on this one. Every shot can benefit from a pre-shot routine. Driving, putting, the long game . . . it doesn't matter. It's just a way to pull the trigger without thinking about it.

To get some hints, just check out men's and women's Tour players. Whenever you're onto something new you always look at the best. I want to look at the best and see how they do it. I don't need to look at somebody I can beat. I want to see the guys I can't beat. How do they do it?

You've got to say, okay, I don't care where the ball goes at first. Then find a routine. Are you going to stand behind the ball to get your line? Find an aiming spot in front of the ball? Walk up from behind the ball? Walk into your stance? A practice swing or two? How many waggles do you want? Two times and then go? Three times and go? Whatever, be certain you do it the same every time. I'm saying you should approach the ball the same way every time on the course *and* on the practice tee.

---

## BIGGEST MISTAKE AMATEURS MAKE . . .

IN MY VIEW THE SINGLE BIGGEST MISTAKE MOST GOLFERS MAKE IS TRYING TO ADJUST OR CHANGE WHAT THEY DO FROM MOMENT TO MOMENT AND DAY TO DAY. REPETITION IS WHAT THIS GAME IS ABOUT. AS SOON AS SOMETHING HAPPENS ON THE GOLF COURSE — OUT OF THE NORM OR UNEXPECTED — THE PLAYER WHISPERS TO HIMSELF, "I'LL CHANGE THIS." NOW HE OR SHE BEGINS TO TINKER AND ADJUST. NEXT THING YOU KNOW YOU'VE GOT MELT-DOWN. ALL SKILLS AND ALL THAT HARD WORK SUDDENLY GO BYE-BYE. CONFUSION SETS IN, FOLLOWED BY ANGER, THEN DESPAIR AND THEN, IN MOST CASES, MENTAL "QUITTING." QUITTING TAKES PLACE WHEN THE SELF-DEPRECATING HUMOR BEGINS. HOW DO YOU GET OUT OF THE MENTAL MESS YOU'VE MADE? THINK ABOUT PRACTICE A. USE THOSE GUIDELINES. TAKE THEM TO THE FIRST TEE ALONG WITH YOUR PRE-SHOT ROUTINE. DO THAT ALL DURING THE ROUND, OR THE REST OF THE ROUND, AND LIKELY YOU WILL PLAY JUST FINE.

Watch the players on the Tours when they are under heavy pressure. Watch a guy or a gal who has waggled the club twice all day and now is under the crunch. After the second waggle suddenly the feet shift, then there's a third waggle. Name your favorite brand of ball and I will bet you a bag of them this shot is going to be trouble. That's because now everything has changed — swing plane, timing, tempo, confidence . . . the whole nine yards.

So keep it the same no matter what. If you could legally marry those things, I'd go buy the ring right now. Because the mind doesn't know what's happening. If you do the same thing over and over again — on the practice tee and on the golf course —  you can fool the body into ignoring pressure. Gotcha that time, Brain!

There has to be a consistency. We're talking about a way to get your game from the practice tee to the golf course here. If your routine on the golf course is totally different from what you do on the practice tee . . . well, has your practice been effective? As we used to say back in my home town, "No way, San Jose."

When you practice, always use your pre-shot routine. Don't just machine gun golf balls out there. Set up for every shot on the practice tee with a pre-shot routine, then use that same pre-shot routine on the golf course. Trust me — are you ready for this? — this is the secret of getting your game from the practice tee to the first tee. If there is a better way, I don't know it. You won't

. . . One last look at the target to "feel" alignment . . .

find yourself mumbling yet again the golfer's tired lament, "How come I can hit the (bleep) ball the so well on the (bleep) range, but can't buy a (bleep) swing out here on the (bleep) golf course?"

Tom Watson played at Stanford when I played for San Jose State. Back then Watson had a real quick up-and-down motion behind the ball before he took it back. That was his waggle. It looked like a piston engine. When he first came on Tour, he changed that waggle. Now it is longer, back and forth over the ball. But it is still a quick-pace waggle.

119

. . . Then comes the takeaway, thinking only tempo, balance and target.

There is a blood relationship between waggle and tempo. Show me someone who has a quick, short waggle and I will show you someone who has a quick, short swing. Show me a long, languid waggle, and I'll show you a person who has got a long, flowing swing.

Davis Love III had trouble with his putting tempo early on. Now and then the putter would be jerked back. That wouldn't work. And he knew it. So he decided to develop a pre-shot routine with his putting stroke. Why not? And

it worked. Davis has become one of the best putters out there.

But I'll guarantee you that when Love started practicing this pre-shot routine with his putter in his hands, the goal was not for the ball to go into the hole. I guarantee that before it finally felt comfortable, he had to go through the agony of missing a mile of putts. But he stayed with it.

His intention was to look at the hole once. Then, as his eyes returned to the ball, down the line of the putt to the ball, the putter started in motion. That was his routine. He did not want to stand over it and lock up. He did not want to do that to himself. The idea was to look once at the hole, then eyes back at the ball and the stroke sort of just kicked in automatically.

He committed to it and turned it into a habit. Now he doesn't have to think about it. The larger point is, you have to put in your time to make it all happen without so much as a single thought. Sorry, no short cuts. And, yes, it is perfect practice that makes perfect, remember?

There are golfers on Tour who have problems with a waggle or pre-shot routine, usually the more expressive players. Maybe a Seve Ballesteros, a Lee Janzen or a Jesper Parnevik. Instead of a waggle, they kind of feel their way to moving the ball around in a direction. Guys like this are decidedly target-oriented. They don't pay much attention to the technical side of the game. I don't think Seve has ever had a technical thought in his life.

A guy I never thought had a particularly good pre-shot routine is Nick Faldo, because he always seemed to go about each shot differently. Subtle, but perceptible. He's always doing something different in his takeaway, always monkeying with what he does before he sets the club in motion to make a swing. So it's seldom consistent. It may be consistent today, but rarely all week or from week to week.

Repetition is the name of this game. For men, for women. For young players, for seniors, for righties and lefties. For everyone. As I have said before, you really aren't going to be able to change your swing that much with a lot of technical advice from teachers and books. The thumb print! Face it, most people physically cannot duplicate what the David Leadbetters of the world are asking you to do. But you can "get game" out of practicing a pre-shot routine. I mean, it will help you tremendously to lower your scores.

A guy with a great pre-shot routine is Tom Weiskopf. He was always on the same beat. Always. The right foot would go down to begin the address, then the left foot. Nicklaus is another who has a great pre-shot routine. Always the same.

Mark O'Meara was a guy who didn't have a real effective pre-shot routine early in his career. But after working with Hank Haney awhile, he developed a very long, lazy waggle in an effort to rehearse his takeaway. In 1998 it finally paid off handsomely. He won two majors.

Learning a pre-shot routine is the best way, I believe, of getting your swing and game from the practice tee to the golf course, one way to solve one of golf's great contradictions — that practice does not necessarily make perfect. It is the Range Rat's dilemma. You are out there beating ball after ball, grooving mistakes, and your scores stay the same or even get worse.

True Range Rats will tell you they've had some strange experiences getting their games from the range to the first tee. It's an old story. They find something in their swing on the range and they start hitting the ball just super. Then they "cross the road" to the first tee, and that same swing sends the ball sideways. Absolutely sideways. It's as if there's some kind of weird zone between the range and the golf course. Passing

## BEST PRE-SHOT ROUTINES . . .

- BILLY CASPER
- JACK NICKLAUS
- TOM WEISKOPF
- MARK O'MEARA
- TOM WATSON
- FRED COUPLES
- DAVIS LOVE III
- AMY ALCOTT
- NICK PRICE
- LAURA DAVIES
- PAYNE STEWART

through that zone to the first tee is like suddenly parachuting into Bulgaria, or someplace totally unfamiliar. *Twilight Zone* stuff.

At the Olympic Club in San Francisco for a photo session for this book, I met for the first time an otherwise pleasant, normal fellow, John Flanagan, on Olympic's magnificent range. "Flan" has a black belt in Range Ratting, his Olympic buddies say. He is out there every day, hitting as many as 1,500 balls a week and exchanging golf stories and swing ideas with his fellow Rats. Decent swing, a little quick, a tad flat. On the range I watched him hit some good-looking shots. But he doesn't play much golf, he told me. But why?

He calls the golf course "The Dark Side," and to venture there is to risk being carted off by the guys in the white coats, he says most seriously. How bad is it? Well, let's put it this way: He is right-handed, but he putts left-handed, cross-handed and sometimes with his eyes

closed. Bad. Real bad. I had no idea what to tell him, other than maybe spend a couple of months with sports psychologist Bob Rotella. Flan had no pre-shot routine. No sign of one. And you could not pay me to watch him putt.

So, you say everything works just fine on the range? Hard to figure, isn't it? I can't say I've been where Mr. Flanagan has been — to "The Dark Side" — but I know all about suddenly losing my swing or hitting a streak of lousy putting. Been there.

Yet somehow I have always found ways to practice this game with methods specifically designed to get me and my game out of harm's way. Yes, I freely admit I have had to endure prolonged on-again, off-again slumps that landed me on Bob Rotella's couch. I hope Flan will read this book, work on establishing a pre-shot routine for every part of his game, including putting. He will chase away those demons. Guaranteed.

# Chapter 8

## BAD THOUGHTS AND BUMMERS . . . KILL 'THE COMMITTEE' . . . SERIOUSLY, TRY TO HAVE A GOOD TIME OUT THERE . . .

The time came that the tournaments I played in as a junior golfer got increasingly more serious. Stuff happens. Things change. It was playing in those tournaments where I first noticed that the fun can take a holiday. There was a finality that came with walking off the last green. The results could not be changed. Dreams and ambitions had been put on hold.

Not so at the range. There I could still try things and my enthusiasm for the game usually would return. I could hit as many buckets of balls as the next guy. I enjoyed that. It was in the "becoming" that I loved most about golf. That was always there for me on the range, it seemed. I would nearly always leave a practice session pumped up about *my* game and *the* game. There was no finality to practice. The range

was a great place to make friends, especially for a kid. The range was cool.

There was no "committee," which is what I call all that needless negative feedback we golfers give ourselves, those little voices in the back of the head that preach doubt. A committee usually slithers into your life about the time you begin to think you are bulletproof. It can happen to junior players. It can happen to pros.

The committee can show its smarmy face when you wake up in the morning and your mind is a blank. Right there at the foot of the bed, that committee can wait for you like a bad debt. It says, "Oh, you awake now? Well, we want to tell you exactly how you have failed."

And then it slaps your face a couple of times and reminds you of your carelessness and misjudgments from the day before. You missed the cut, stupid. We told you so. You failed yesterday and you will fail again next week because you are a gutless, low-rent, bottom-feeding dweeb. Plus you are ugly. Your clothes don't match. People find you disgusting. Your swing sucks. You look like a total fool around the greens. You walk funny and you eat with your mouth open. Scrap everything and start over, four-putt breath!

You can't be a golfer at any level, either gender, and fail to recognize what I am talking about. I call it "the committee." By any other name it is doubt and self-abasement, the arch enemies of confidence and optimism.

I remember even my father sometimes would come home sullen from a Saturday round of golf played poorly. He would just sit there and suffer.

Golfers do that to themselves. If we don't play to the level we think we should, we allow ourselves to suffer. Sadly, some even wallow in it.

I read a funny line that perhaps makes my point. "Just once," a golfer says to himself, "I wish I could play my usual game."

Ben Hogan once said it was funny how he only remembered the bad shots. That's the committee. See, even Mr. Hogan knew doubt.

When self-imposed expectations are not met, bet the rent the committee will be there first thing in the morning to explain it all to you.

That voice never existed inside my head on those youthful summer evenings. Rather, the voice I heard as a kid was,

## RANGE WEIRDNESS . . .

- JOHN DALY HITTING A DRIVER OVER THE GALLERY.
- ARTIE MCNICKLE HITTING A CADDIE WITH A BALL.
- LEE TREVINO BRINGING A PLASTIC SNAKE OUT OF HIS BAG.
- TREVINO IN HAWAII HITTING THE SECOND ZERO OF A 100-YARD MARKER WITH ONE SHOT.
- PAUL BLANCHARD IN A GORILLA SUIT.
- PHIL MICKELSON HITTING A SAND WEDGE BACK OVER HIS HEAD.
- JOHNNY MILLER HITTING MORE THAN ONE BUCKET.
- TIGER WOODS ALONE ON THE RANGE.
- BRUCE LIETZKE'S CADDIE PUTTING AT BANANA UNDER A HEAD COVER.
- JUSTIN LEONARD WITH HIS CLUBS OUT OF ORDER.
- THE HILARIOUS THINGS PLAYERS SAY TO AN IN-FLIGHT GOLF BALL.

A great golf range like Olympic's has a snack shack and a place to rest (background). I strongly recommend rest and relaxation after about 40 minutes of practicing before going at it again.

"Wow! You can do this!" Everything was wonderment and imagination. I felt joy playing the game. And it *is* a game, you know.

For me, the game begins on the range. For me, this is where the fun starts. I have been fortunate enough for most of my career — but not all of it — to be able to carry the wonderment and fascination, the hope and competitive fervor, the challenges and the mystique of the game, all this with me to the golf course.

Sure, there's hard work to be done if you intend to stay competitive. But digging divots isn't exactly digging ditches.

There was a time in my life that this game had become exceedingly difficult. From 1978 to 1983, I felt as if I were being attacked by giant fire ants every day on the golf course. I was beat up. The committee had pitched a tent in my head. I was consumed by the notion that I should be better than I am, wishing that one more time "I could play my usual game." I was working hard, it seemed, but without any signs of improvement.

Then I met famous sports psychologist Bob Rotella. His first question to me was, "What is the difference between you now and you when you were younger and playing well?"

I told him when I was a kid I didn't have a care in the world. If I played well today, fine. If I didn't, fine. No worries. He asked me to name the changes I have seen in myself from my boyhood.

I have grown up a little, I said. I

think I am more diligent. I carry myself in a professional, responsible way, I think. Stuff like that.

"Well," he said, "what makes you think you were so wrong to be the other way — carefree and fun-loving? You are playing a game. Now you just happen to be playing it for a living."

So my goal in 1984 was to have fun, to recapture that game I played on those splendid summer evenings. You talk about something easier said than done — get out on the golf course and start not letting it get under your skin that you had somehow lost "it." What I wanted was to be able to leave the golf course each day and tell myself that, hey, that was fun. The way I used to do.

Taking your game from the practice tee to the first tee is no different for a player on the Tour than it is for anyone else. The problem is all about playing right into tension and then not being able to finish the job.

Anyway, a funny thing happened on my way to oblivion. My scores started getting better. I started competing again. I could complete tournaments. I started to have genuine fun, not some exercise in self-deception. I was getting out of my own way and letting myself play.

No matter how hard you practice, if you can't get this down there is no hope. You have to learn how to get out of your own way.

The committee said, "Look, if you're just going to have fun out there, we're not sticking around."

# Chapter 9

## CELEBRATING TRUE RANGE RATS . . .
## TALES FROM THE TOUR . . .
## THE NEW BREED . . .
## CHECK OUT THIS TRUE STORY . . .

Often I have read and heard media critics complain that the Tour doesn't have colorful, interesting players anymore. Those critics should get out of the press tent and hang out on the range. That is where the Range Rats hang, of course. In that milieu there are — pick your cliché — a lot elevators that don't go all the way to the top.

Colorful? Well, I'm the only guy I know who can win a tournament and lose the first-place check in a bar. But I'm not alone in the colorful department. There's a whole pack of us out there.

Whether I have a mike in my hand as an NBC golf analyst or a bag over my shoulder as a player, when I check in at a tournament I always go to the range first. And it's not necessarily to prac-

tice. The driving range is where we hang, the place to catch up on what's been happening. It is our home away from home.

You may think the locker room is the place where Tour players gather to break each other's chops, but that is not the case at all. In the locker room we are all very much individuals. We are there getting to the golf course and preparing for the day's play, or we're taking off our golf shoes and getting ready to get back to our families again.

But a Tour range is different. Most of us are out there looking for the camaraderie, news, rumors, inside stuff, golf talk, and for certain a few laughs. I have long held that it is the best part of the Tour. I would bet that players on the women's Tour and the Senior Tour feel much the same.

If there is one thing I know about practice, it's that you're good for only

127

**The cursed red stripe painted on the range ball means two things: One, you are not on a great range, and two, the paint will end up on the face of your club.**

about 40 minutes, where you can really focus and hit ball after ball. Then if you are at least half-bright, you will take a break. You need to get away.

Sometimes you go down to the end of the range to tell stories, hear the one-liners and spend time to get to know your competitors. And that's when a guy will say, "Will you take a look at me? Where's my alignment?" It is an interesting dichotomy. Pro golf is a game at which you spend all day trying to beat each other's brains out, but then on the range a competitor is asking you for help. You give it without hesitation.

You know he would do the same for you.

The range is the only place where we are all in this together, part of the traveling road show. Sometimes we just kick back and tell stories. I love that part.

Like my first encounter with the new breed of Range Rat. It was one of those pro-am deals where they put me on a par-3 hole and I hit a shot with every group that came through. Then this one guy comes by and tees up a ball with a big red stripe around it. I just kind of looked at the ball, then sort of checked him out all over to see if the fellow might be in need of a few weeks in a golf hospital in the lip-out ward.

The guy had a pretty good swing. He was well dressed and looked the part of having been around the game a while. He seemed to know what he was doing, except for the driving-range ball. With the red stripe on it.

After he hit the shot I asked why he was hitting a range ball.

"What do you mean?" he asked. I pointed out that the ball he just hit had a big red stripe on it. He said why, yes, right over there at the practice tee you could buy 60 of those specimens for only a couple of bucks. He practiced with some, then kept the good ones. Let's see, those probably would be the balls with the freshest red paint, wouldn't you say?

Okay. Uh-huh. Right. Wow, nobody's gonna believe this one!

This guy was that new breed I had heard about — the Range Rat who had never been on a golf course. I had thought most of them were in Japan, where golf courses are scarce and drop-dead expensive, and three-decker driving ranges are scattered like Seven-Elevens.

This chap might have been through four sets of clubs that never saw a golf course. One thing for certain: He loved driving ranges. But he was a Range Rat through and through. You have to give him that. He fit the mold.

A Range Rat is someone who really gets into practicing this game, and through that experience blends into the RR culture. We work in the laboratory of golf, the place where quirky types make breakthroughs, where innovation and new philosophies are trotted out and shared. Range Rats are the backbone of golf, where the culture of the game is truly celebrated. One more eccentric shouldn't be disquieting.

There is a guy I know who complained about a new range they built at his municipal golf course. He said the sun is always in his eyes. Doesn't like it one bit. Bad design.

So I asked him what time he hits balls. He said before he goes to work every morning. Now I ask him if he has ever been there in the afternoon or evening. No, he says. Well, that sun moves, you know. The earth rotates . . . oh, never mind.

"Strange" fits. It's part of a Rat's charm. Strange also rhymes with Range, so I guess we can make room for Strange Range Rats. Maybe we could call our more severe cases the Deranged Rats. Sometimes strange is a simple matter of historical perspective.

It may seem strange to those who haven't followed the Tour for the last couple of decades — or even to some of the younger pros on Tour — that we

---

## SIGNS I'D LIKE TO SEE POSTED ON A RANGE . . .

- "DON'T HIT TOWARD THE GALLERY."
- "HIT FIRST ZERO (100 YARDS) FOR FREE BUCKET."
- "FREE VIDEO OF YOUR SWING."
- "DON'T USE RANGE BALLS ON COURSE."
- "HIT OFF GRASS, NOT MATS."
- "SEEK PROFESSIONAL HELP."
- "JUNIOR GOLFERS WELCOME."
- "TODAY'S BEST STORY FROM THE COURSE."
- "HIT 300 SIGN FOR FREE CHIROPRACTIC SESSION."
- "FREE ADVIL."
- "FREE DRINK WITH THIRD BUCKET."

used to carry our range balls with us wherever we went.

When I came out on Tour, that is the way it was. We had our own portable range. Sound strange? Well, we took it most seriously.

It was called a shag bag. And it was the most important piece of equipment we carried with us, outside of our clubs. Our range in a bag. And we never let that leather bag out of our sight. It was our briefcase, our way of doing business.

We practiced with our own golf balls for good reason. Few courses as recently as 25 years ago had decent practice facilities. If they did, they usually had those solid range balls that were hard as a rock. You know, the ones with the red stripes. That's not what a Tour pro needs for practice. We need the same feel we get when we play, the same feel as the wound ball we use on the course. So we practiced with the same balls we used on the course, the balls in our precious shag bags.

Because we all used our own practice balls, the caddies would have to shag balls for us out on the range. There would be all these guys hitting balls and an equal number of caddies out there on the range shagging them. Caddies were the aiming point. When we changed clubs, we would wave him to move back or forward a little.

It was something to see, about 50 or 60 caddies standing out on this range, each trying to shag his player's golf balls. All over the range you could hear, "Incoming left." Or, "Incoming on top

of you." It was golf's version of a mortar attack.

That all ended around 1977 at Pensacola when Artie McNickle — we called him "Crazy Artie" — dropped a caddie. Artie hit this flaming low duck hook that nearly took out a platoon of caddies. A guy named Irving got the worst of it.

That did it. Shagging balls on Tour with caddies was over. Now the ball manufacturers provide them for free. Brand new every week. Gross upon gross.

It was unsettling at first to travel the Tour without a shag bag. I have mine still. If you see a golfer with a shag bag these days, now there is your Range Rat.

There are a lot of guys on Tour who hit a zillion balls on the range. But some are not real Range Rats, in my book. Take Vijay Singh. Nobody practices longer than Vijay. He's out there until there are no more balls or darkness takes over. He is the kind of guy who's vexed when the sun goes down. He counts the hours until he can get back to beating balls. Doesn't make him a Range Rat, though.

Singh always goes all the way down to the right end of the range so his back is to everybody. Though a nice fellow, he really doesn't want to deal with people. He is there to work. He is not there to chat. Now to me, that's not a Range Rat.

A true Range Rat is Lee Trevino. If there were a Hall of Fame for Range

Rats (not a bad idea, really), Lee's statue should be the tallest. When he was playing the Tour and healthy, Lee would work hard out there, don't get me wrong. But he had a needle that could reach six hitting-stalls left and right. Always had a joke, a new story to tell, an opinion on an issue, some way to break the tension.

Range Rats come in all shapes and sizes, as people would in any other culture. Lee was special, and still is on the Senior Tour. If you taped his mouth shut he couldn't break 80. That's just the way he is. And a lot of the things he has said and done through the years are legendary Rat stories.

Like the time in Hawaii. At the Hawaii Open, we play at "0 Dark :30,"

as soon as the sun comes up. Literally, you get to the golf course and it is still dark.

This one morning Trevino showed up late. Overslept. And he was teeing off in a few minutes. So he's running on down to the range saying he is late and telling no one in particular that he's got to get going. Then he takes an open spot next to Tom Watson.

Watson says, "Okay, Mex, show me something."

Lee had not hit a ball yet, not one shot. He was still tying his shoes.

"What do you need to see?" Lee inquired.

And Watson said, "Hit the 100-yard sign."

"Give me something tough. That's

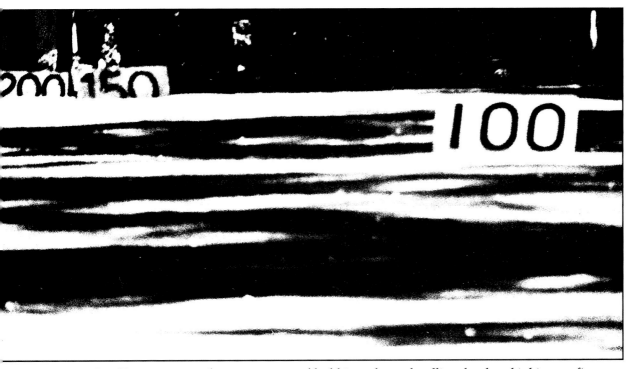

Lee Trevino, in a rush to warm up, grabbed his wedge and, calling the shot, hit his very first shot in the middle of the second zero, then ran off to the putting green, declaring himself ready. This story is legendary on the Tour.

## A BAD RANGE HAS . . .

- NO TARGETS, JUST AN OPEN FIELD.
- MATS ONLY.
- LIMP FRENCH FRIES.
- MUSCLE GUYS IN TANK TOPS.
- NO TRUE RANGE RATS.
- ALLIGATORS (FLORIDA).
- NO LOANER CLUBS.
- NO SHORT-GAME PRACTICE AREA.
- REALLY BAD GOLF BALLS.
- BALLS WITH PAINTED STRIPES AND THE PAINT GETS ON YOUR CLUBS.

too easy. Tell you what. I'll hit the right zero," Trevino chirped.

Everybody's watching by this time.

"To do that, though, to hit that right zero, I'm going to have to knock it down and turn it over a little bit right to left," he said.

His first shot hit smack in the middle of that right zero on the 100-yard sign. The players on the practice tee stood silently, thunderstruck, as if they had just witnessed some improbable event, like the sinking of the Titanic. Writ large on every countenance were the words, "Did . . . you . . . see . . . that?"

"It doesn't take long to warm up a Rolls Royce," Lee hollered over his shoulder as he trotted off to the putting green. His only practice warmup was that 100-yard wedge. There you have it: Perfect practice does indeed make perfect.

I remember a young pro coming up to J.C. Snead, wanting to ask him a question about his swing. The young pro said he thought J.C. had the best waggle in golf. He asked J.C. if he would teach him the waggle.

J.C. looks down at the ground. He appeared to be upset.

"Waggle?" J.C. says, as if he had just been harpooned. "Oh, man! Am I doing that again?"

I talk as much as anyone. There's just something about the range that feels like home. That also makes me a target. I'm not immune to a lot of those stories that go around the range. Stories about me have been going around the range for a long time. Doesn't bother me. They're all true.

Like the time I won in Boston. And lost the check.

It was my first year on Tour, 1975. I had won the Quad Cities the week before Boston, but I just barely made the cut at Pleasant Valley in Boston. Made the cut right on the number. The next day in high winds I shot 66 and leapfrogged everybody.

On Sunday morning, I just got the feeling I was going to win. I don't know why. I know nothing about those vision and déjà vu deals. But I didn't have a credit card back then, so I figured I'd better get some money. So I cashed a check for $600 that morning.

Then I won. That's two in a row. Pretty good.

And on the 18th green, the man who ran the tournament — his name was Cuz — handed me a surprise. Usually they give you that big dummy check when you win. But Cuz gave me the real check during the presentation. On the Tour I had never received a real check. What do you do? You fold it up and put it in your pocket, right?

So I go back into the clubhouse, buy a few rounds for the guys in the bar. Then I went to my courtesy car, where Dick was waiting for me. He was my personal driver. Real nice guy. So I asked him where you go in this town for a good time. He recommends this place called T.O. Flynn's in downtown Worcester. An Irish joint. No shortage of those in Massachusetts.

Next thing I remember is waking up the next day. I sat around the edge of the bed forever, thinking about how lousy I felt. And then two things kind of dawned on me — I won yesterday, and I had been over-served last night. But two wins in a row, that's a pretty good reason to celebrate. Now I thought I would go down to the lobby and buy a newspaper and read all about myself.

In golf there is a saying about being cocky — it's that warm, comfortable feeling that comes over you just before you make double bogey.

So I slap on the pants, reach into the pocket. I don't have a dime. I've got nothing. No cash, nothing. Now what do I do?

Then I remember. They gave me a check. And I don't have it.

So I call back to the golf course, got Cuz on the phone. I told Cuz I had a certain a problem. He laughed like hell. Not to worry, he said. Payment on the check will be stopped. They would replace it. Then I realize I have no cash. No credit cards. Can't even get out of town.

So I called back and asked good old Cuz if he would give me a thousand in cash and just make the check out for $39,000. I never really did get that $40,000 first-place check. I got $1,000 in cash and 39 K with a new check. Meanwhile, at the bar they found my check when they were cleaning up. On the floor it was.

The owner of the bar had called me. I told him payment on the check had been stopped and he could keep the check or throw it away. He then wanted to know if he could frame it. No problem. So, I guess there is an Irish pub in Massachusetts with my $40,000 check still hanging on the wall.

Ken Venturi was my hero as I was growing up. I played golf at San Jose State on a Ken Venturi Scholarship. When Ken was at SJ State his head coach was the guy who taught me the game of golf, Eddie Duino, head professional at San Jose Country Club.

Ken had been on the Tour, but he was in a slump. He came to put on a clinic at San Jose CC for us and played a round. I was probably Eddie's hottest student at the time, so he introduced me to Ken. A very big moment for me.

Venturi gave me one of his golf balls and signed it. I remember it all so clearly. It was a Royal LP Special. LP for Long Play, like a phonograph record. He signed it with a ball point pen. That ball went right on my dresser. And stayed there.

A couple of years later Ken was slumping, having a tough time. It was right before the U.S. Open at Congressional. I sold him out.

I had a junior tournament at the time, but I needed a new ball to play with. I looked at that ball on my dresser, down it came, wash cloth came out, off came the "Venturi" and I put the ball into my bag.

And then I lost the ball on the course.

Two weeks later Ken won the Open at Congressional. That was the Open in

which the doctor told him if he went out in the afternoon he might die of heat prostration. I was happy for my hero Ken, but I was kicking myself for losing a ball signed for me by a U.S. Open champ.

I also lost a gallery post. Now, that is not easy. I have not the slightest idea where it is.

In 1976, Hale Irwin and I tied for first after 72 holes in the first Memorial Tournament, the one created by Jack Nicklaus. Ken Venturi had given me a lesson the week before, and I broke out of a slump. Hale and I were in a three-hole playoff, starting on the 15th.

We both birdied, then we both made pars on the 16th. Now came the fateful 17th. Hale knocked his shot in there about six feet from the stick. I pulled my 4-iron badly and it sailed way left, above

## DUMBEST THINGS AMATEURS DO ON THE RANGE . . .

1. GRABBING THE DRIVER FOR THE FIRST SWING OF THE DAY.
2. CHANGING SWING ON A WHIM.
3. NEVER PICKING A TARGET.
4. LOOKING AT GOLFERS AT NEARBY STALLS AND EMULATING THEIR SWINGS.
5. RABBIT EARS — TRYING A "TIP" FROM A GUY GIVING A LESSON IN THE NEXT STALL.
6. NOT LINING UP PROPERLY. OR, NOT LINING UP AT ALL.
7. IGNORING THE WEDGE.
8. NOT FINISHING A SESSION WITH A WEDGE TO GET THAT SLOW, EASY TEMPO BACK.
9. GUESSWORK.
10. HITTING WHILE TIRED.

the green. But the ball hit this metal post that was holding the gallery rope, bouncing straight back onto the green, close to the hole. We both missed our birdie putts, so now we go to the 18th hole and sudden death.

Hale hit his drive into the trees and had to knock it out across the fairway. I made birdie and won the tournament. At the awards ceremony they gave me the gallery post that saved my butt on No. 17.

Lost it. Have no idea where it is.

To this day the guys on the range needle me about the gallery post or the check I lost, players who were boys at the time.

Now, why should I think a guy playing a red-striped range ball on the golf course is strange? He's a Range Rat. Just one of us.

*By Shannon Rouillard*

# Grab a spot, girl, and hit away!

Except for the professional ranks and college kids, there just are not many bonafide Range Rats among women golfers. I am a Range Rat, and I am proud to be one. But I would feel much better if I could recruit some of my "sisters" to join the clan.

Too many of my female students tell me they don't like to practice because they feel intimidated by all the men who seem to make the ranges — public and private — their second homes. A woman also may feel she does not belong there because her swing still is in the fundamental stages.

Nonsense, I tell them. Quite a few men on the public and private practice ranges are in varying stages of development themselves. So go grab a spot, girl, and hit away! See it as a way of inspiring other women to do the same, and as a way of saying, "Lookout, men! We are excited about getting better at golf and we're going to be good!"

Practice, practice, practice . . . to the majority of us it is not the most fun activity, but it can be if we know how to practice efficiently so we can take our practice results to the golf course.

That is why I think this unique book by Roger Maltbie is such a terrific idea. I love his explanations. And, frankly, his illuminating thoughts on practicing are new to me, too. Women should use his charts in this book, and from them learn what to practice and how to practice. No more guesswork. With careful attention, your charts will tell you exactly where your deficiencies are.

As a teaching golf professional, I can say readily that one of the most common questions I am asked is, "How can I take the 'range' to the golf course?" My experience as a competitive player has taught me that there are many answers to that question.

First of all, you cannot be afraid to practice. You cannot let yourself be intimidated by a bunch of men on the range, then try to practice fearlessly yourself. The two don't mix.

You must work on your weaknesses regularly. If you want to see real improvement and become a better player, you have to enjoy "grinding" away on the practice tee. Face it, you have to become a Range Rat, like me. But I love the game so much I have made it my life's work. Anyway, to complete the point, I am saying that to improve you have to put aside those feelings of dread of practicing. That goes for men, too.

Once women get past the fear barrier, then they really can begin to enjoy their practice time. This is essential to getting better as a player, as Roger points out several times in this book. You must learn to love going to the range. "Range Rat" is just the colorful name Roger uses to express the determination and passion it takes to improve.

Practice to improve your game, but also relish the imagination and experimentation, and the self-examination that comes with true Range Ratting. There is much more to derive from practicing than improved ball-striking. You are also learning how to play, how to get your game from the range to the golf course. And you are meeting new golf friends of both genders — fellow Range Rats — who are struggling with the same challenges that you are trying to meet.

You must practice with a purpose. What I mean by this is, we must practice the way we want to play. Whether you are on the range or on the putting green, you need to have a target and you must go through your pre-shot routine for every practice shot. Roger brings this out splendidly. I recommend you read those parts very carefully. Twice, perhaps. You will learn that in golf it is not practice that makes perfect, but "perfect practice that makes perfect."

Let me emphasize the need for you to be positive. Be your own best friend. Play within yourself — don't try to hit shots you haven't already practiced on the range.

You must practice your swing or technical points offered by a teacher. Separately, you must practice how to play the game as well. This means, among other things, that you must hit to targets and mentally picture your shots. Before you hit the ball, see it fly and land where you want it to land.

Once you have become a Range Rat like me, do not forget to practice and focus on your short game — pitching, chipping, sand play and putting. This area of the game cannot be emphasized enough, especially for women. The reason for this is because most women are not able to hit many greens in regulation. A refined short game can mitigate long-game problems and produce better scores.

The whole point behind the "Range Rat" term is to express humorously that practice must be frequent and fun. That is, if you really want to take your game with you to the first tee.

# Golf Lessons Galore . . .
# Show Me The Greenery . . .
# Remember Which Pro Teaches
# Which Swing . . .
# A Range Rat's Paradise . . .

*By Bill Scott*

How many times have I found my swing on the range but left it there? Hundreds of times. How many times have I hit the ball super on the golf course but scored poorly? My good-score rounds come only when I "grind," it seems.

On those rare occasions when I forget about the swing and the range and simply play golf, more often than not I get the ball onto the green and make pars and birdies. But I keep leaving my game on the range. It does not want to go to the first tee with me. What causes this? "Why?" I ask myself over and over.

Then, invariably, I think, "Lesson, lesson, go take a lesson." I have faith that, perhaps with enough lessons, the day will come when the playing of the game becomes the true end for me. That is my objective, I tell myself. I try to believe it.

But until that time — forgive me this line — I am home, home on the range. I am a classic Range Rat, I know it. I always will be driven to go to the range. Again and again. To experience the delight of hitting those white golf balls from lush, green grass for periods without boundaries is very close to the sustained comfort I seek.

The game of golf has many attractions. Competition and comradery in generally peaceful and often beautiful settings are spoken of as the primary factors in this addiction so many of us share. But to me, the aspect of this wonderful experience that continues to grip me is the contentment found on the golf range. Here one can strive to get better, even though somehow the journey always is better than the destination. Life is good.

There is something mystical about a golf range. Thanks to chance and good fortune, for most of my 45 years of golf I have been permitted to enjoy more than my share of mystical, magical golf ranges.

A golf or practice range is not a driving range. A "driving range" generally is found beside some busy thoroughfare next to a shopping center or on an otherwise deserted country road.

Often a driving range has more than one level. The hitting areas have worn, greenish-brown plastic mats. Rubber tees stick up through holes in the mats. You get golf balls from ball dispensers. Rectangular yardage signs and an occasional flag dot a dusty, fenced-in expanse.

Someone patrols the landing area in a ball-collection vehicle that resembles vehicles created for traversing moonscape. The golf balls come in prism shades — yellow, orange, pink, even purple. They often have stripes. And rocks aren't that hard.

A golf range is connected to a golf course. The ideal golf range is spacious, tree-lined and grass-covered. Golf is green. The hitting area on a golf range is moved daily so that a fresh strip of thick green grass is always available. The divot patterns created by the golfers at the range are precise and gathered together in square or rectangular shapes. The immediate hitting area is identified by taught ropes, generally yellow, drawn from one side of the range to the other. The balls are relatively soft and remarkably white. No stripes. They are stacked in perfect order, sometimes resembling white pyramids.

There are many great golf ranges. My golf travels have enabled me to have particular affection for two: Pine Valley in Clementon, New Jersey, and Muirfield Village in Dublin, Ohio. Other outstanding ones I love are Bent Pine in Vero Beach, Florida, the Tournament Players Club in Jacksonville, Oyster Harbors on Cape Cod, Olympic Club in San Francisco, Ridgewood Country Club in New Jersey and Saucon Valley in Bethlehem, Pennsylvania.

These golf ranges and clubs rank among the best in the county. There is, however, no direct relationship between quality of course and quality of range. The golf range at Pebble Beach is a joke, as is the one at Baltusrol — two legendary U.S. Open venues. You can have a super golf course without having a super golf range but it would be silly to have a super golf range without a super golf course.

The time I have spent on golf ranges probably exceeds the time I have actually spent playing golf. Most golfers only go to the range as the preliminary step to the golf game ahead — to warm up. Some also go to the range after playing golf to correct swing flaws revealed during the round. I do both, but mostly I go to the range because there I am free to hit golf balls in quiet seclusion for the pure pleasure of feeling that solid hit and watching the flight of the ball against a blue sky to a landing place not as carefully selected as it should be.

I have, on many occasions, driven three hours not to play golf but to hit balls at one of my mystical golf ranges. I make such treks certainly to practice but mostly to be at the range for two or three hours of hitting irons, woods and bunker shots, and to do some pitching and chipping — not putting.

I do not like putting. Ben Hogan was right. Golf in reality is two games — striking the ball and putting. I seek perfection in the hitting part of the game and care little about the putting part. A friend suggests strongly that this attitude could have a correlation to my scores. I scoff.

My golf and my accompanying love affair with the golf range began when I was 16. My dad got me started. At Ridgewood High School in northern New Jersey, I played football, basketball and baseball and was a mediocre pole vaulter.

My father recognized before I did that my athletic career would end with high school. He suggested that I find a sport which I could play for the rest of my life. He identified two such sports — tennis and golf. The year was 1953 and Ben Hogan was more well-known than Jack Kramer. I choose golf. Easy call.

Dad told me that he would pay for six starter lessons. My choice of golf, made with no thought or research, turned out to be life-shaping. Forty-five years of playing, taking lessons and falling in love with a good range have followed a choice made with all the instincts and introspection a 16-year-old kid could muster. Not a whole lot, in other words.

My game never reached the level the time spent would seem to demand. I have tried to qualify for several USGA events, but as yet have never passed the requisite qualifying tests. I have come close to qualifying for the U.S. Amateur, the U.S. Senior Open, and the U.S. Senior Amateur. Being close is painful.

I have won three club championships at two different golf clubs and one Senior Invitational Tournament. My greatest golf triumph was winning the Pine Valley Member-Guest with four Walker Cuppers in the field. In that event, I had an exceptional partner — not a Walker Cupper — who played well and carried me along. I can play a little, but I still get dusted too often by my weekend cohorts.

I have taken more than of 250 golf lessons — that's a conservative number — from more than 40 different teachers. This accounting does not include trips to a three-day session at Jim McLean's school at Doral, a three-day session at Peter Croker's school at Hilton Head and a three-day session at Dave Pelz's short game school in Austin. I have two golf-crazed sons who attended the Jim McLean and the Peter Croker schools with me. When you consider the cost of these lessons and the cost of trips to take lessons, well, I try not to think about it.

The six starter lessons my dad arranged laid the foundation for my golf and started my fascination with golf ranges. My first teacher was Yazo Consalvo, the golf pro at Saddle River Country Club in Paramus, New Jersey. Saddle River was a public course — such courses for some reason are now called "daily fee courses" — and Yazo was a local institution.

Yaz taught me the fundamentals of grip, setup, weight transfer and turn. I don't remember the specifics of those first lessons, but I recall vividly the pleasantness of the experience. The days were warm, the ground soft, the grass green, and Yaz was both patient and kind.

In college at Brown University, my football, basketball, baseball and pole vaulting days were history. But I did make the Brown golf team. I was not a good player, by any means, but Brown didn't have a good golf team. I played in every match during my junior and senior years. We played our home matches at two wonderful courses,

Wanimoisett and Rhode Island Country Club. Each had forgettable golf ranges.

Two years active duty in the Marine Corps followed college. The time was post-Korea and pre-Vietnam. The Second Division, to which I was assigned, had a golf team for which I played. We were good Marines but not very good golfers. We traveled to various bases for matches and I even qualified for the All-Marine Tournament at Parris Island in 1960. Phil Rodgers, at one time a winner on the PGA Tour and now a respected teacher, was then a wise-ass PFC who played in that tournament and finished third.

In September, 1961, I was due to end my service and begin law school. The 1961 All-Marine was to be played early in October at Camp Lejeune, home of the Second Division and my home course. I came close to extending my military career by one year to play in that tournament. Was I hooked on golf, or what?

At Camp Lejeune, my fascination with golf ranges grew. Lejeune's range was certainly not mystical but it was in close proximity to my room in the Bachelors Officers Quarters. After a day in the field, I would rush to the BOQ, change clothes and head for the range. As the sun was setting, I would hit ball after ball, pausing occasionally to smoke a cigarette.

It was cool to smoke in those days and I tried to emulate Arnold Palmer in smoking, hitching my trousers (not pants, girls and sailors wear pants, Marines wear trousers), and striking the ball. Over the next few years, my law practice provided my growing family with enough resources to move from our apartment to a house. It also enabled me

to join a super golf club, Columbia Country Club in Chevy Chase, Maryland. One of the attractions at Columbia was that it had the legendary Bill Strausbaugh as its golf professional.

My first lesson with Bill (affectionately called "Coach") soon grew to more, and a lasting friendship developed. Today, 27 years later, Bill, who is now retired and pro emeritus at Columbia, on occasion watches me hit balls on the Columbia range. Lesson fees were never important to Bill. His encouragement and advice to me were always given with little interest in payment. The PGA probably would not approve.

The golf range at Columbia is not a mystical range. It provides an adequate setting for taking lessons and talking golf with playing buddies. The grass is sparse and there are too many of those plastic mats that should be, but are not, used only for bad weather and off-season practice. The range is too small and too close to Connecticut Avenue, a busy street. It is definitely not peaceful.

Two of Bill's former assistants, Dennis Satyshur and Jim Fitzgerald, have played prominent roles in my Range Ratting life. Dennis, now the head pro at Caves Valley outside Baltimore, and Jim, now the head pro at Chevy Chase Club, right outside Washington, D.C., have given me more lessons than I am sure they want to remember.

By a wide margin Dennis is the leader in the number of lessons given to me. These lessons were taken at Columbia, at Pine Tree in Florida (a super range), Bent Pine in Vero Beach (a super range), Baltimore Country Club (an adequate range), and Caves Valley (a super range — Caves has mats but they

141

are surprisingly grass-like.) Each year, Dennis would have a new swing thought he would try to convey. My few golf accomplishments were under Dennis' guidance.

Once I even took a lesson from him over the phone.

Jim Fitzgerald ranks right behind Dennis in the number of lessons given to me. These lessons were taken on the Chevy Chase range which ranks high among ranges in quality and beauty. The trouble with Chevy's range is that so many nonplayers use it. On the mystical golf range one finds wonderful ball-strikers with strong, fluid swings — not the lashes and lunges of the most the members.

A significant problem in taking lessons from three different professionals, close to each other geographically and professionally, is that you must remember where you are when you are playing or practicing and being observed by one of the three. Dennis and Jim teach different methods than does Bill, despite their being tutored in lesson-giving by Bill.

Their swing concepts are different. I try to remember to use Bill's methods when at Columbia, Jim's methods when at Chevy Chase, and Dennis' methods when at Caves Valley. The worst possible scenario is for me to use Jim's or Dennis' methods while being observed by Bill. It is only when I retreat to the splendid isolation of the golf range that I can use my method of choice for that particular day. My pals say I have been too long in the sun.

Bill's successor at Columbia is Bob Dolan, himself a terrific teacher. Aware of my love of ranges, he has visited with me on the Columbia range on countless occasions,

imparting encouragement and advice. Humor accompanies all of his comments, which makes our sessions extra enjoyable. One year, when Bob and I played in the Pine Valley pro-member, we avoided the cocktail party following our round and instead took to the magnificent Pine Valley range where we hit balls until sunset.

One other young professional who has had great influence on my golf life is Jack Bohman of Cape Cod National. I first met Jack when he was my opponent in the finals of the Club Championship of Eastward Ho! on Cape Cod. That was 20 years ago. Jack was in college still. Despite the embarrassment of losing to me in that match, Jack turned pro soon thereafter. He's a much better player now and one of the best young teachers I know.

My lessons have occurred in many states and at many golf ranges. I have taken lessons from young and old professionals, from men, and from women. Yes, I took a lesson from Louise Suggs, the legendary LPGA Tour player. My chauvinist golf pals think this is funny. But my sainted wife Jane is proud of me.

Consistency in teaching apparently is not required by the PGA. I have been told to stand close to the ball and stand away from the ball. I have been told to use an overlap, an interlocking and a baseball grip. I have been told to hold the club in a death grip and to hold the club as if it were a little bird. I have been told to retain the angle and to get rid of the angle. I have been told to move my head back and to keep my head still. I have been told to have passive hands and to fire my hands. I have been told to drive my legs and to forget my legs. I have been told to shut the club face and to open the club face. I have been told to make contact with my back to the target and to make contact when square to the target.

All this contradictory advice would seem to suggest that golf lessons are a waste of time and that I am crazy for taking so many conflicting lessons. Not so — I am convinced there simply is no one answer. Look at Lee Trevino, Arnold Palmer, Tiger Woods, Jim Furyk, Fred Couples — different swings, great players.

In the mid-1970s one of my clients asked me if a friend of his, a struggling touring pro from Escondido, California, could stay at our house during the Kemper Open. Which then was played at Congressional Country Club in Bethesda, Maryland, about five miles from our house. Our home was populated then by four kids in their early teens, my wife Jane, me and a lazy old dog. I, of course, said yes. A touring pro in our house for the Kemper? Are you kidding? Jane and I will sleep in the car if necessary!

His name is Gary McCord. Although he never did much at the Kemper, he became a part of our family for Kemper week for the next six years. More times than not, he failed to make the cut and ended up playing over the weekend with me and two of my pals. For Gary, those weekend rounds must have been agony. For me, I hung on his every word.

For the time Gary would stay with us for those wonderful six years, our house became an entertainment center. Gary is a stand-up magician. He amazed us with his card and coin tricks. One evening we went to dinner at a restaurant where performers did magic tricks. I knew the owner and asked him if

Gary could perform. He agreed and Gary wowed the audience to the chagrin of the other magicians.

Gary was great to our family and still comes to see us when he returns as a famous television personality and a Senior Tour winner. He helped my golf game immensely while also making sure my head stayed in the real world.

On evenings after dinner, he would accompany me to the Chevy Chase range and watch me hit shots. I was so pumped. "Keep your day job," he would say, or, "You can forget the Tour, Billy." He showed me how to hit better bunker shots and how to chip better. He is a first-rate teacher. What you see and hear on television is the real thing.

Another lesson I took from a "famous" professional was from John Schlee, who nearly won the U.S. Open in the 1960s. When I met him, he was a teaching professional at Monterrey Peninsula Country Club in California. The setting was beautiful and the course was great. The range was awful.

From John Schlee I learned nothing. He was a gentlemen, but I could barely understand him. He talked about kinetics. I still don't know what kinetics are. I struggled through my half-hour nodding my head to signify I understood what he was saying. I kept wondering if this lesson would ever end.

Finally, he said, "Have you go it?" Oh, sure, I said. Down pat. I beat a hasty retreat, thinking I might be doomed in my search for the perfect hit. But I continue my pursuit to this day.

Every golfer has been told somewhere along the way to find something that works and stay with it. No argument from me. I accept it. I believe it. I cannot do it. It simply is too much fun to continue my quest for that one thing that works. It's the struggle, not the achievement, that is the reward.

My sons, Billy and Tommy, have come to love the game nearly as much as I do. Once they thought that my preoccupation with golf ranges was silly. Now, they're not so sure. When they were younger, my calls to them to come to the range with me were less like invitations and more like commands.

Many a summer's evening my sons and I would go to Columbia's range when it was closed and hit my own shag balls until dark. We all three hit shot after shot. When darkness prevented further ball-striking, we would search in the near blackness to find my precious shag balls.

Billy was a Marine officer in Desert Storm. He has become an excellent player. Tommy is half of "Tom and Tom Juice Guys," who have given the world Nantucket Nectars. But I still see them trying to catch my shots in my shag bags. They would try to position the shag bags under my falling shots and make basket catches. I reasoned that this seemingly dangerous activity was good for their hand-eye coordination. We ceased the practice when Tommy misjudged the path and rate of descent of a well-struck 7-iron and took the full impact of a Titleist on his chest. The imprint of the Titleist lasted several days. Back at home, the saintly Jane was decidedly unclear on my hand-eye concept.

My ideal range is the one at Pine Valley. I envision heaven as a place not unlike that golf range. I picture the scene . . . Two hours of daylight remain. A slight right-to-left wind is blowing. My sons are somewhere down the line ignoring my occasional tips.

My requests of them to watch a few of my swings are granted, although the expected praise is not forthcoming. My dad, using his wooden driver, is hitting tee shots 150 yards but straight.

My lifer playing partners, Ned Longson, Glenn Mitchell, Geoff Robertson, Bobby Abbo and Dave Burgin, are on the range doing their things. Super golfers Gordon Brewer, Bill Shean, Burke Hayes and Jack Vardamann are carving out the ideal divot patterns that only real Range Rats know how to create.

The click of iron to ball and the thud of iron to turf are interspersed with the splat of metal driver to ball. Everything is green. The four or five flags on bunkered greens at various distances from the hitting area move slowly in the easy breeze — the perfect wind for ball-striking, according to Ben Hogan.

Despite my many lessons, I am poor at giving tips or observing. I cannot translate a professional's advice to someone else's golf swing. My usual comment is "slow down." The thought usually is ignored, anyway.

By now I have reached a mental state that is difficult to explain here, but I will try nonetheless. I become a sportscaster, you see. I am broadcasting my own performance in the U.S. Open. It might go something like this: "Young Scott . . . out of Brown University . . . known for his work ethic . . . learned his classic pre-shot routine from the book by Roger Maltbie . . . young Scott's fellow players call him 'The Range King' . . . this 6-iron is critical if he is to win the Open . . ." My Range Rat colleagues and kin all turn to watch. The pressure on me is huge.